Editor-in-Chief and Founder:
Lyndon H. LaRouche, Jr.
Editorial Board: *Lyndon H. LaRouche, Jr. , Helga
Zepp-LaRouche, Robert Ingraham, Tony
Papert, Gerald Rose, Dennis Small, Jeffrey
Steinberg, William Wertz*
Co-Editors: *Robert Ingraham, Tony Papert*
Technology: *Marsha Freeman*
Transcriptions: *Katherine Notley*
Ebooks: *Richard Burden*
Graphics: *Alan Yue*
Photos: *Stuart Lewis*
Circulation Manager: *Stanley Ezrol*

INTELLIGENCE DIRECTORS
Economics: *Marcia Merry Baker, Paul Gallagher*
History: *Anton Chaitkin*
Ibero-America: *Dennis Small*
Russia and Eastern Europe: *Rachel Douglas*
United States: *Debra Freeman*

INTERNATIONAL BUREAUS
Bogotá: *Miriam Redondo*
Berlin: *Rainer Apel*
Copenhagen: *Tom Gillesberg*
Lima: *Sara Madueño*
Melbourne: *Robert Barwick*
Mexico City: *Gerardo Castilleja Chávez*
New Delhi: *Ramtanu Maitra*
Paris: *Christine Bierre*
Stockholm: *Ulf Sandmark*
United Nations, N.Y.C.: *Leni Rubinstein*
Washington, D.C.: *William Jones*
Wiesbaden: *Göran Haglund*

ON THE WEB
e-mail: eirns@larouchepub.com
www.larouchepub.com
www.executiveintelligencereview.com
www.larouchepub.com/eiw
Webmaster: *John Sigerson*
Assistant Webmaster: *George Hollis*
Editor, Arabic-language edition: *Hussein Askary*

EIR (ISSN 0273-6314) *is published weekly
(50 issues), by EIR News Service, Inc.,
P.O. Box 17390, Washington, D.C. 20041-0390.
(703) 297-8434*

European Headquarters: *E.I.R. GmbH, Postfach*
Bahnstrasse 9a, D-65205, Wiesbaden, Germany
Tel: 49-611-73650
Homepage: http://www.eir.de
e-mail: info@eir.de
Director: Georg Neudecker

Montreal, Canada: 514-461-1557
eir@eircanada.ca

Denmark: EIR - Danmark, Sankt Knuds Vej 11,
basement left, DK-1903 Frederiksberg, Denmark.
Tel.: +45 35 43 60 40, Fax: +45 35 43 87 57. e-mail:
eirdk@hotmail.com.

Mexico City: EIR, Sor Juana Inés de la Cruz 242-2
Col. Agricultura C.P. 11360
Delegación M. Hidalgo, México D.F.
Tel. (5525) 5318-2301
eirmexico@gmail.com

Copyright: ©2018 EIR News Service. All rights
reserved. Reproduction in whole or in part without
permission strictly prohibited.

Canada Post Publication Sales Agreement
#40683579

Postmaster: Send all address changes to *EIR*, P.O.
Box 17390, Washington, D.C. 20041-0390.

Signed articles in *EIR* represent the views of the authors,
and not necessarily those of the Editorial Board.

Turn the Flank

The Institutions Have Failed: We Must Make All Nations Great Again

by Michael Billington

> Together, let us choose a future of patriotism, prosperity, and pride. Let us choose peace and freedom over domination and defeat. And let us come here to this place to stand for our people and their nations, forever strong, forever sovereign, forever just, and forever thankful for the grace and the goodness and the glory of God.
>
> —*U.S. President Donald Trump to the UN General Assembly, Sept. 25, 2018*

Sept. 25—President Donald Trump used the occasion of his speech to the United Nations General Assembly today to utter a clear and unambiguous defense of the individual national sovereignty of every nation, as well as the right of those nations to a future of peace, economic development and prosperity.

As to be expected, media coverage declared that the speech was a reiteration of Trump's alleged "America First" outlook,—thus attempting to smear the President by linking his views with the U.S. Nazi sympathizers of the 1930s—but for those who heard or have read the speech, what stands out is Trump's *charity* toward other nations, and his insistence that these nations all have the right to develop as sovereign powers, in cooperation with their neighbors. He repeatedly stressed the crucial importance of the culture and values of each and every nation in bringing about peace and development internationally. As he said in regard to the horror of the drug gangs and human traffickers in Ibero-America: "Ultimately, the only long-term solution to the migration crisis is to help people build more hopeful futures in their home countries. Make their countries great again!"

Trump's Own Words

Excerpts from the President's speech provide a vivid picture of his vision:

EDITORIAL

Each of us here today is the emissary of a distinct culture, a rich history, and a people bound together by ties of memory, tradition, and the values that make our homelands like nowhere else on Earth.

That is why America will always choose independence and cooperation over global governance, control, and domination.

I honor the right of every nation in this room to pursue its own customs, beliefs, and traditions. The United States will not tell you how to live or work or worship.

We only ask that you honor our sovereignty in return . . .

Many countries are pursuing their own unique visions, building their own hopeful futures, and chasing their own wonderful dreams of destiny, of legacy, and of a home.

The whole world is richer, humanity is better, because of this beautiful constellation of nations, each very special, each very unique, and each shining brightly in its part of the world.

In each one, we see awesome promise of a people bound together by a shared past and working toward a common future.

As for Americans, we know what kind of

future we want for ourselves. We know what kind of a nation America must always be.

In America, we believe in the majesty of freedom and the dignity of the individual. We believe in self-government and the rule of law. And we prize the culture that sustains our liberty—a culture built on strong families, deep faith, and fierce independence. We celebrate our heroes, we treasure our traditions, and above all, we love our country.

Inside everyone in this great chamber today, and everyone listening all around the globe, there is the heart of a patriot that feels the same powerful love for your nation, the same intense loyalty to your homeland.

The passion that burns in the hearts of patriots and the souls of nations has inspired reform and revolution, sacrifice and selflessness, scientific breakthroughs, and magnificent works of art.

Our task is not to erase it, but to embrace it. To build with it. To draw on its ancient wisdom. And to find within it the will to make our nations greater, our regions safer, and the world better.

To unleash this incredible potential in our people, we must defend the foundations that make it all possible. Sovereign and independent nations are the only vehicle where freedom has ever survived, democracy has ever endured, or peace has ever prospered. And so we must protect our sovereignty and our cherished independence above all....

When we do, we will find new avenues for cooperation unfolding before us. We will find new passion for peacemaking rising within us. We will find new purpose, new resolve, and new spirit flourishing all around us, and making this a more beautiful world in which to live.

So together, let us choose a future of patriotism, prosperity, and pride. Let us choose peace and freedom over domination and defeat. And let us come here to this place to stand for our people and their nations, forever strong, forever sovereign, forever just, and forever thankful for the grace and the goodness and the glory of God.

Thank you. God bless you. And God bless the nations of the world.

Breaking Free from Imperial Rule

This issue—of freeing the nations of the world from (in President Trump's words) "global governance, control, and domination"—is the paramount issue of our time. One thing that distinguishes the LaRouche political movement, is that we have insisted that this phenomenon of "domination" be addressed by its accurate name—the British Empire.

For over fifty years, Lyndon LaRouche has identified the crisis facing mankind in the 20th century, and still today, as the existence of the legacy of imperial institutions, set up and run by and for the benefit of the British Empire and its financial institutions.

These British imperial bodies include the wretched World Trade Organization (WTO), enforcing "free trade" policies which function to keep the former colonized nations in perpetual poverty, never achieving industrialization. It also includes such imperial courts as the International Criminal Court (ICC), used exclusively to punish African and other developing nation leaders who refuse to follow the dictates of their former colonial lords. It includes many of the agencies of the UN itself, parading as "human rights" enforcers, but actually used to justify economic and military interventions against sovereign states, under the imperial "responsibility to protect" doctrine of former British Prime Minister Tony Blair.

After sixteen years of Bush and Obama subservience to London, there is finally an American President who has the courage to take on those institutions, and to insist that mankind can do better. Just as President Trump has stuck to his insistence that the U.S. should be friends with Russia, so also has he openly rejected the British "globalization" hoax, designed to sustain the Empire, and has enraged the British and their assets in the U.S., who are running a British coup attempt against the President. Their panic is clear, as the overt role of the British in that coup attempt, identified by LaRouche and *EIR* from the beginning, can no longer be hidden.

George Papadopoulos, one of Robert Mueller's targets, just last week blew the whistle on the British and their "Five Eyes" control over the set-up of Trump. On Sept. 24, the former U.S. Attorney for Washington, D.C., Joseph diGenova, said on WMAL radio that "the U.K. is at the center of the conspiracy to frame Donald Trump and Carter Page and George Papadopoulos," pointing to both MI6 and GCHQ, which he identified as "the head intelligence operation out of the U.K."

Trump has pointedly rejected the free trade pacts, the "global warming" hoax, the ICC, the "human rights" mafia, and the "East versus West" imperial divide—all created by the British to impose the dictates of the City of London and Wall Street over the rights of sovereign nation states. Defending these rights, which were the fruit of the 1648 Peace of Westphalia and the European Renaissance, requires the final end to Empire, and to the geopolitical thinking behind it.

LaRouche PAC Intervenes

On Sept. 25, the LaRouche Political Action Committee (LaRouche PAC) held a rally at the UN, welcoming delegates from around the world with a beautiful poster reading, "Blessed Are the Peace Makers," with pictures of Trump shaking hands with Vladimir Putin, Xi Jinping, and Kim Jong-Un.

Although a great deal of noise has been made in the media about Trump's criticisms of Iran and his claims that its government sponsors terror and suppresses its own people, it is important to recall that in his speech last year at the same UN event, Trump railed against "Little Rocket Man" Kim Jong-Un as a threat to humanity. This is Trump's style. In a tweet on Sept. 25, he said that Iran's President Hassan Rouhani had not accepted his invitation to meet, but, "Maybe someday in the future—I am sure he is an absolutely lovely man." President Rouhani, on his side, said in his speech that dialogue is possible and necessary, while also denouncing Trump's rejection of the Iran nuclear deal signed under Obama. Such a dialogue is required if the festering crisis across the so-called Mideast is to be re-solved—not piece by piece, but comprehensively, with the Syrian crisis and the Israeli-Palestinian conflict included. This would deprive the British of their primary "cockpit for war," just as the Korean peace process has foiled imperial efforts to force Asian nations and others to "take sides," rather than joining together in the Spirit of the New Silk Road.

The LaRouche PAC rally also distributed the petition titled, "The Leaders of the United States, Russia, China and India Must Create a New Bretton Woods!" The petition underlines the pending explosion of the financial bubble in the trans-Atlantic region, as well as the growing panic in Europe as the EU itself is falling apart. It is LPAC's intervention in this area of economic and financial policy which is both singular, and absolutely vital to the ultimate success of the Trump Presidency.

In his UN speech, President Trump took credit for the expansion of production and job creation in the United States during the last two years. Yet some of President Trump's recent public remarks tend to blur the distinction between the stock market and the real economy, and this may come back to haunt him, especially if the stock market bubble explodes before the crucial midterm elections. This threat could be resolved if Trump were to act now, with the other nations of the "Four Powers" and others that choose to participate, to prepare to convene a New Bretton Woods conference, to implement the necessary international reorganization of the financial system along Hamiltonian lines, as presented in LaRouche's proposed Four Laws.

This truly will secure sovereignty and economic well-being for every nation on Earth.

EIR**Contents**

www.larouchepub.com Volume 45, Number 40, October 5, 2018

**Cover
This Week**

Frederick the Great addresses his generals before the Battle of Leuthen, Dec. 5, 1757, during the Seven Years War.

TURN THE FLANK

DETROIT TOWN HALL

LaRouche PAC in Michigan: Stop the Coup and Win the Future!

This is the edited transcript of opening remarks by Susan Kokinda and Ron Kokinda to the LaRouche PAC Town Hall of Sept. 29, 2018 in Northville, Michigan in the 11th Congressional District just outside Detroit.

Susan Kokinda: Welcome to the LaRouche PAC meeting. I'm Susan Kokinda. We are now less than six weeks away from the very decisive and history-making midterm elections, that will determine whether or not the nation, and the world, will move forward with Donald Trump's Presidency and Lyndon LaRouche's policies, or whether we are going to be dragged into an impeachment process, and back to the Obama/Bush policies of perpetual war, regime change, and economic disintegration, which will accelerate when the Western financial bubble bursts, which could be very soon.

With the Brett Kavanaugh hearings this week we have all seen that the enemy will stop at nothing to destroy the institutions of this nation. I'm sure our special guest speaker Barbara Boyd will be addressing this as an element of the ongoing coup process. Our job, your job, is to lift the population above the screaming, of the media, and of partisan politics.

The LaRouche PAC Pledge

As many of you know, on Aug. 17, the LaRouche PAC released a Policy Statement titled, "Countdown to the 2018 Mid-Term Elections: We Must Take Charge Now!" identifying the midterm elections as the most crucial elections perhaps of our lifetimes. That statement calls on *citizens* such as yourselves to take charge. We can't let the media, we can't let the political parties set the agenda. We have to set the agenda.

This statement calls on candidates to adopt three pledges. In other words, there are three standards to which we have to demand that those running for office rise to, and I want to read those three pledges to you:

1. I will not support impeachment of President Donald Trump. In general, I will act to end the ongoing insurrection against the President and to investigate those responsible, referring them for prosecution where warranted.

2. If elected, I will undertake to implement Lyndon LaRouche's four principles for the urgent economic recovery of the United States....

We list those principles, and all of you will have copies of this leaflet, so I'm not going to read the details of that.

And finally,

3. I will work with Russia and China and other nations on areas of mutual interest, particularly conquering terrorism, joint ventures to develop infrastructure for the world's developing economies, and exploring space. President Trump has attempted this program for peace. He has been blocked at every turn by the City of London and Wall Street and politicians who profit from perpetual war and the cheap labor regimes of globalization....

I'm happy to report that we actually have our first United States Congressional candidate in the country who has endorsed this statement, and he's right here in Michigan! It's Jeff Jones, the Republican candidate for Congress in the 12th Congressional District (CD). He's running against incumbent Democrat Debbie Dingell, who replaced her husband John Dingell, when he retired from Congress. That's the district which runs from Downriver all the way over to Ann Arbor. I think we have some of Jeff's constituents with us today.

He has endorsed our campaign. We have welcomed

his support, and we have urged the voters in his District to take his campaign with the utmost seriousness, and also obviously to understand the disastrous consequences of a Democrat-dominated Congress. We invited Jeff to come today—but, not surprisingly, he's campaigning in his own District, which this isn't. He has sent greetings to our meeting, and my husband Ron will read those greetings.

Ron Kokinda: I had the opportunity to attend a "Meet the Candidates" evening on Tuesday. Jeff Jones, who is running for U.S. Congress from the 12th CD, invited people to come in and meet candidates and to make some remarks. From the 14 State House Districts and 8 State Senate Districts that overlap the 12th CD, there were three candidates for the Senate, three for the House, and also a Supervisor candidate, along with a Republican official for southeast Michigan. Jeff introduced me as with the LaRouche PAC, an organization that can give you a very good idea of what's going on behind the scenes.

Statement of Jeff Jones

Here is Jeff Jones' statement to our meeting. It was dashed off in haste, so it may be rough in spots:

Dear Fellow Patriots of the LaRouche PAC,

It is with great pleasure, I send you greetings!

Who would have ever guessed that we would be seeing what we are seeing in the political kingdom? These distractions on progress are quite the oxymoron!

It is amazing how black becomes white and white becomes black, the very core philosophies of Luciferianism developing around us.

So what is Fascism? What is Prejudice? What is Progressive? What is Machiavellianism? What is Liberty, for that matter?

As our Constitution is now raped publicly without defense, it is the rallying in the voter's booth that becomes our deliverance!

As a Regional Vice President in Financial Services, I thought there is no way we would ever see the Dow rise about 12,000? 15,000 would unsustainable?

Right??? 20,000, miraculous, and yet suspect! But to be thinking 30,000 even possible is

Jeff Jones, Republican Candidate for U.S. Congress from Michigan's 12th CD.

a completely different world than the last century!

Educational Renaissance is my top platform issue because it becomes the nucleus of our economy, our social justice, and the empowerment of a nation!

If we can undo 100 years of educational meltdown, we can revive an appetite of greater vision for all of the community.

Although NAFTA was destructive to the 12th district, it was a temporary treatment to a failing auto industry. The management of its successes and planned failures are now just being realized.

As the Silk Trail slowly gets rebuilt, and the reassuring of a genuine global economy, we may find a balance of trade, but more importantly, an opportunity of stabilization to index.

As our President restores prosperity to Americans and takes control of foreign policy, it is only those who have sold out to private legacies that are fearful of his strategies. Protecting our alliances and exposing our enemies is a light that many hope to be put out!

My role in Congress is, uphold our Constitution, and have the insight to shore up leadership that lasts long after I have served.

Unfortunately, Congress has become a power seat, a lobbyist's wet dream, and our nightmare!

Thank you for the many LaRouche team members that have friend requested, shared my posts and videos, and are encouraging me, while in the trenches moving forward. Collectively, we become a bigger community of visionaries.

Please help our team in the defeat of dynasty politics, selfishly controlled industry pockets, and the hindrance of genuine progress. Tell your friends of the 12th to go to www.facebook.com/jeffjones4congress and share my weekly videos and posts to exponentially outreach and expose to all we hold dear, the flaws of the last 50 years of decay. My 14 grandchildren, and your children's children, are depending on you! God Bless you and the citizens of the United States that get the benefits of visionaries like yourself!

Sincere thanks,
Jeff Jones,
GOP Candidate,
U.S. House, MI-CD-12

We Witness the Birth of a New Movement

Susan Kokinda: I want to highlight something Jeff said, because I think it points in a very important, new political direction, and that is, you notice, he said he's campaigning against the failed policies of the past *fifty* years—not the last eight years, but the past fifty years. In other words, he's addressing a much more systemic failure, and looking for policies that will give us a future.

Similarly, John James, the Republican candidate for United States Senate, is a military veteran and a businessman. He was recently asked at an event, how does his family feel about him running as a Republican? He's African American, so the assumption was, his family is all Democrat. And what he said was: "The Democratic Party abandoned us a long time ago." But he has further gone on to say that both political parties have failed us.

I think what we're seeing with actually viable candidates who are out there, is that they're using the Republican Party as a vehicle, as Donald Trump did. But this is a new phenomenon in the country. There is an independent movement under way, and this underscores our role. This election is not about politics, or parties, it's about a new policy and a new paradigm.

I do want to bring to the attention of our audience,

besides, that there are two other independent candidates in the country, who have been endorsed by LaRouche PAC: One is Ron Wieczorek, an Independent running for Congress from South Dakota, and the other is Kesha Rogers, whose campaign is our national flagship campaign. Rogers is running as an Independent in the Texas 9th CD in Houston, against one of the leading proponents for impeachment, Democrat Al Green. She's about to get her first billboard up, outside Houston, and we're going to make her campaign a national spearhead, to show people how to fight; that you can't duck the impeachment issue.

The midterm elections are all about Donald Trump versus an Impeachment Congress. It is not about the individuals, in most races. There are some clearly qualified, unique people, who are affiliated with us. In many other cases, you may look at the Republican candidate

EIRNS

LaRouche PAC organizing in Detroit, Michigan, September 2018.

and shrug—but that's not the issue! The issue is, will there be an Impeachment Congress, or a Congress which won't get in Trump's way?

So, without any further introduction, I want to turn the discussion over to Barbara Boyd. Barbara is the Treasurer of LaRouche PAC. She is the author of our famous dossier on Robert Mueller, *Robert Mueller Is an Amoral Legal Assassin: He Will Do His Job If You Let Him.* If you don't have that dossier yet, get one.

Ms. Boyd has headed LaRouche's legal defense team, engaging in head-to-head battle with Robert Mueller, when he indicted Lyndon LaRouche in the 1980s. So I think it's safe to say that Barbara is the nation's leading veteran in the fight against Robert Mueller. Please welcome Barbara Boyd. [applause]

BARBARA BOYD

Concerning the Fate of the Nation
Address to the LaRouche PAC Town Hall in Detroit

This is the address of LaRouche PAC Treasurer Barbara Boyd to a LaRouche PAC meeting in Detroit, Michigan, on Sept. 29, 2018. Her prepared remarks have been edited.

In Augustine's *Confessions*, he tells the story of his student's addiction to the killing games of Rome. Alypius, Augustine's student, protested to his friends:

'Though you drag my body to that place and set me down there, you cannot force me to give my mind or lend my eyes to these shows. Thus I will be absent while present, and so overcome both you and them.' ... But when one of the combatants fell in the fight, a mighty cry from the whole audience stirred him so strongly that, overcome by curiosity and still prepared (as he thought) to despise and rise superior to it no matter what it was, he opened his eyes and was struck with a deeper wound in his soul than the victim whom he desired to see had been in his body.... For, as soon as he saw the blood, he drank it in with it a savage temper, and he did not turn away, but fixed his eyes on the bloody pastime, unwittingly drinking in the madness—delighted with the wicked contest and drunk with blood lust. He was now no longer the same man who came in, but was one of the mob he came into, a true companion of those who had brought him thither.

We are, as a nation, involved in a

cspan

Supreme Court Nominee Judge Brett Kavanaugh testifying at his Senate Judiciary Committee hearing, at which Democrats focussed on alleged sexual assault, Washington, D.C., Sept. 27, 2018.

color revolution, a cold coup against the President, and, I will argue here, against reason and truth and this nation itself. Many of us, for the past few days, found ourselves, as in Augustine's account of Alypius and the Roman killing games, glued to a televised spectacle in

Painting by Jean-Lé Gérome

"The Christian Martyrs' Last Prayer."

the United States Senate, involving the President's nomination of Brett Kavanaugh to the United States Supreme Court. To slay this nomination, Democrats and their media allies tossed aside the most fundamental legal principles of this Republic: the presumption of innocence; the necessity of evidence and corroboration to establish and prove accusations; due process; actual cross-examination of the accuser; and the deliberate search for truth.

Andrew McCabe

These principles were replaced by Gladiator Senators, pretending to defend all who have been abused and raped, if not all womanhood besides. The first half of Percy Bysshe Shelley's poem, "The Mask of Anarchy," is a fitting reference for the horror, fraud, and hypocrisy which we are all witnessing. Tell me, does anyone even remember or know what kind of judge Brett Kavanaugh is, or what his judicial philosophy is? Think about that as the Coliseum crowd, our national news media, demands that you opine about things they say he did at the ripe old age of 17. Thumbs up! Thumbs down! In this new Roman world we have inhabited since the 2016 election, that's all you have to do to claim your title as citizen.

But I will argue to you today that the Kavanaugh hearing of Sept. 27 was actually a turning point, and the color revolution and "Resist" have made a fatal error in overreach, even if an error whose magnitude will not at first be apparent.

The past two weeks have seen key events in reversing this coup: (1) There is increasing recognition that the British instigated the coup. (2) The President has ordered a rapid declassification review of key documents in the coup which will expose the British hand. That is why the British had a hissy fit about President Trump's order to declassify the Carter Page FISA Warrant, the Bruce Ohr 302s, and key text messages among the top echelons of the FBI. It is said that this declassification will also be highly embarrassing and legally challenging for the CIA and John Brennan. (3) A *New York Times* leak on September 21 revealed that at meetings involving Deputy Attorney General Rod Rosenstein, who has been quarterbacking the Russiagate investigation against Trump, there was discussion of using the 25th Amendment to the Constitution to oust the President, and of Rosenstein wearing wires to record his conversations with the President. These meetings occurred shortly after Donald Trump fired FBI Director James Comey in May of 2017.

Yesterday, the House Judiciary and Government Oversight Committees, which are jointly investigating illegalities associated with the coup, worked out a deal for Rosenstein to appear imminently to tell them about this treasonous May meeting—who was there and what was said—and they are subpoenaing the memos of fired FBI Deputy Director Andrew McCabe about this meeting and others. McCabe's memos were the source of the *Times* story.

Rosenstein, of course, had a better idea than the very faulty 25th Amendment gambit. He almost immediately appointed Special Counsel Robert Mueller to execute the intent to take down the sitting President.

So, on the one hand, I will give you an update on developments in the coup, in which the Kavanaugh hearings are an integral part. And I will again tell you, that a key determining point in the coup is the upcoming midterm elections on November 6. How we portray these journalists and Democrats between now and then, the people who have become nothing but anarchists and madmen, slick peddlers of sick lies—how we ridicule their ignorance of the most fundamental principles of our Constitutional Republic, and whether we make that ridicule stick, may very well determine the future of this Republic.

But my second topic is an even more important one. In her Schiller Institute webcast of Sept. 27, Helga Zepp-LaRouche referenced the means by which the entire mess actually gets outflanked and defeated. With Trump's speech at the United Nations, and his allusion to each nation's developing what Lyndon LaRouche would call "full set economies" for themselves, and the President's intent to make that the basis of international relations, the door is wide open, if we recognize it, for the needed new monetary system. Only under that new system, can mankind actually advance to a higher stage of development.

You see, there is a pervasive error in the analysis of the relations between nations involving trade, which this organization is uniquely positioned to correct. That is because China and certain other nations, as they developed following the 1971 decoupling of the dollar from the gold reserve standard, were the recipients of thousands of manufacturing jobs from the United States—not because China sought to steal these jobs, but because of deliberate policies developed and implemented by Anglo-Dutch imperial entities, such as the Trilateral Commission and the Council on Foreign Relations right here in the United States.

These imperial bodies called for "controlled disintegration" of advanced sector economies in projects spanning the period of the late 1970s into the early 1980s, and for a form of governance they called "fascism with a democratic face." They even exported advanced technologies and defense systems to China, under their geopolitical theory that China would act as a fatal check on the Soviet Union.

It is one of the great ironies of the present situation that one of the architects of this policy, as it was applied to China, was Michael Pillsbury, the man who, right now, is attempting to destroy Donald Trump's relationship with China's President Xi Jinping, and with it the very possibility of the new monetary system necessary for the full set economic development which can secure all of our futures.

The Status of the Coup and Kavanaugh

In the middle of Shelley's poem, "The Mask of Anarchy," after he shows how anarchy appears in the wake of political murder, fraud, hypocrisy, and a sleeping and initially fearful populace—*hope* appears, first as nothing but a weak vapor in the air, and then as follows:

And the prostrate multitude
Looked—and ankle-deep in blood,
Hope, that maiden most serene,
Was walking with a quiet mien:

33
And Anarchy, the ghastly birth,
Lay dead earth upon the earth;
The Horse of Death tameless as wind

Fled, and with his hoofs did grind
To dust the murderers thronged behind.

I think we are now at such a moment, in the coup which has enveloped this country since Election Day, 2016. We have just witnessed a Judge, smeared and pilloried before the public for an incident which allegedly occurred in high school, in 1982, more than 36 years ago. We are being told that justice and all of the history of Western civilization requires accepting the word of his accuser, without question, without any doubt, with elaborate sympathetic rituals praising her courage, and without ever questioning her character, motives, or background. By her own account, she was a 15-year-old girl, a product of the rich and elite suburbs of Washington, D.C., who appeared at a party, as if out of the air, drank some beer, and was assaulted—not raped, but groped—by two drunken prep school boys, one of whom, she says, was Brett Kavanaugh. Both her parents and Kavanaugh's parents belonged to the same exclusive country club, a place notorious for its elite and segregated policies. She then disappeared into the air once more, not remembering where she had been, or how she got either to this incident or back to her home.

She emphatically remembers the boys laughing at her. She gave different accounts, first saying she feared that Kavanaugh was going to rape her, and then in her televised testimony, that she thought Kavanaugh was going to kill her. She told no one about this incident until a therapy session years later with her husband, in which she had to explain to the therapist and her husband why she wanted two front doors on her house. Conveniently for the woman and the propaganda artists waging the campaign on her behalf, the other boy she claimed was in the room was addicted to alcohol as a young man and has been throughout most of his life. He wrote a book about a rambunctious youth and the prep school both he and Brett Kavanaugh attended.

She went on to become a clinical psychologist, studying and becoming thoroughly familiar with the professional literature about the impacts of youthful trauma on the brain; she participated in women's marches against Trump. By her account, she sent a letter to her Congresswoman in California recounting this incident. The letter got to Senator Dianne Feinstein and the national news media, despite her apparent claim that she wanted to remain hidden. Feinstein recommended lawyers for her, who are warriors for the

cspan

Sen. Dianne Feinstein called a witness alleging sexual assault at the Senate Judiciary Committee hearing of Judge Kavanaugh, Sept. 27, 2018.

"Resist" movement. The woman had a polygraph and was scrubbed and prepped for combat. This college professor who teaches authoritatively most days, was rendered a trembling mass of vulnerability.

No one told the Judge about any of this throughout an otherwise grueling confirmation process, until the last minute—when they sprang it on him, and upon his wife and young daughters—calling him an unhinged sexual predator, a girls' basketball coach waiting to pounce on them, a gang-rapist, and every evil smear imaginable.

The Judge testified to defend himself, telling the truth, emotionally, angry in his innocence: This is a political witch-hunt, not advise and consent, but search and destroy. It is because Donald Trump appointed him; it was revenge by the Clintons because he had worked for Ken Starr; and it is all about power and the midterm elections. He pulled out a calendar documenting every day of his summer in 1982, accounting for every day when Ms. Ford said the incident might have occurred. He endured grueling prosecution from the Democrats about entries in his high school yearbook. Sheldon Whitehouse, a dirtbag Senator from Rhode Island, claimed the Judge's yearbook entries somehow implied anal sex, but the Judge deflated him by noting that the term in question was the normal adolescent joke about flatulence.

No one corroborated the accuser's account. Of the four other people she said were there, all denied that they were there or that any such incident had occurred. Senator Lindsey Graham (R-SC) railed at the hysteria and the attempt to crucify the Judge on national televi-

sion, defending the presumption of innocence, due process, and the requirement for actual facts and evidence—without which, there is, as I said, pure anarchy.

For a moment, the Grand Inquisitors stood there stunned, briefly reminded of their Constitutional duties, looking every bit the way the national media looked as the returns rolled in on November 8, 2016. Then, they returned to gathering the weapons for Kavanaugh's assassination, calling him intemperate and belligerent because he defended himself and his family—an angry personification of the male patriarchy itself.

Oh, by the way, as of this writing, Christine Blasey Ford, the accuser, has raised $550,000 on her "Go Fund Me" page. Purely in appreciation for what she has done, as her lawyers are working for free.

The scientific literature about how completely believable but false memories are created, so that they are believed with 100% certainty, has been developed and demonstrated repeatedly in criminal cases. That is why exoneration occurs so often because of DNA evidence,

cspan

Judge Kavanaugh being sworn in at the Senate Judiciary Committee hearing, Sept. 27, 2018.

which contradicts eyewitnesses. I refer you to the work of Dr. Elizabeth Loftus, who has saved many lives by looking into this.

Now there is yet another FBI investigation of the Judge. While it may help the Judge ultimately, it will never look at his accuser critically, or the information war which has been ginned up and sent out to destroy what appears to be a good man. We have to do that, not in some major new campaign, but by reference to what we already know, and by a ruthless campaign of jokes, irony, and ridicule. And doing so, we will win, because, as I said, I believe that their hand has now been badly overplayed, into a fraud which resonates on very significant levels of human identity.

All of this, as Sen. Lindsey Graham said, is about political power, about control of the Senate. It is an evil sham which seeks to destroy an honorable man and his family. As most know, if the Democrats win the House and the President is impeached, the Senate is the body, under the Constitution, which will determine his fate. If the Democrats, who you just saw go to war on behalf of anarchy, take the Senate, Donald Trump and the will of the voters in the 2016 election are, as we say in the vernacular, "toast."

The Coup

With respect to the other major developments in the coup, the national news media went wild last Monday reporting that Deputy Attorney General Rod Rosenstein was on his way to the White House to meet with Chief of Staff John Kelly, either to resign or be fired. The drama unfolded over a *New York Times* story leaked September 21, which portrayed Rosenstein, the man in charge of the illicit Robert Mueller Special Counsel investigation against Trump, arguing that the 25th Amendment should be invoked to remove Trump from office, and offering to wear a wire to gather dirt on the President.

The meetings in which these statements were made, occurred shortly after the May 2017 firing of FBI Director James Comey by the President. While it is a very short distance from the Justice Department on Pennsylvania Avenue to the White House, media reports about Rosenstein being on his way to a dramatic confrontation lasted for some hours. Finally, White House Press Secretary Sara Sanders read an official statement, saying that, "At the request of the Deputy Attorney General, Rod Rosenstein, he and President Trump had an extended conversation to discuss the recent news stories. Because the President is at the United Nations General Assembly and has a full schedule with leaders from around the world, they will meet on Thursday when the President returns to Washington, D.C."

This did not prevent Democrats from going wild and declaring that Trump was engaged in a "slow

CC/Internet Education Foundation

Deputy Attorney General Rod Rosenstein.

moving" Saturday night massacre like President Richard Nixon's firings of DOJ officials.

There are several overlapping dynamics at work here:

1. It is clear that Rosenstein attended a meeting of top FBI and DOJ officials in May 2017, in which invoking the 25th Amendment to remove Donald Trump from office and wearing wires to set the President up was discussed. The *Times* story asserts that Rosenstein advocated this course of action. Rosenstein denies it. His denial, however, really does not matter, because he never reported these treasonous conversations, acting instead, in the wake of the firing FBI Director James Comey by Donald Trump, to appoint Robert Mueller to conduct an unprecedented and *ultra vires* counterintelligence investigation of the President of the United States.

As constitutional scholar and lawyer Alan Dershowitz has repeatedly pointed out, invoking the 25th Amendment in these circumstances amounts to declaring a coup d'état in the United States. Nothing less is implicated by the *New York Times* story. According to several reports, Rosenstein concluded after the *New York Times* story came out, that he could not testify to Congress about these meetings and keep his job, offering his resignation on Friday.

There is now a widespread recognition that

there is an ongoing coup against the President, which threatens the governability of the United States itself. Sen. Lindsey Graham, speaking on multiple media channels on Sunday, September 23, called it a "bureaucratic coup d'état." Many Republican stalwarts and the President's attorneys also recognize that Robert Mueller is a legal assassin, not the embodiment of legal rectitude as portrayed by Washington, D.C.'s best public relations shops.

2. The British are screaming about Trump's September 17 declassification order regarding several foundational documents central to the coup and exposing the British hand in the matter. Trump's declassification order came in the week when George Papadopoulos began talking about the CIA and British efforts to entrap him and fabricate evidence against the Trump campaign, efforts which provided the pretext for the FBI's unprecedented and completely unfounded counterintelligence investigation of the Trump campaign.

The stages of this operation have become very apparent.

There was an initial stage, like the LaRouche case, in which evidence was fabricated by intelligence agencies to be fed to law enforcement. This stage went forward during the Presidential campaign itself, from roughly February-July of 2016 and involved multiple entrapment efforts—many of which

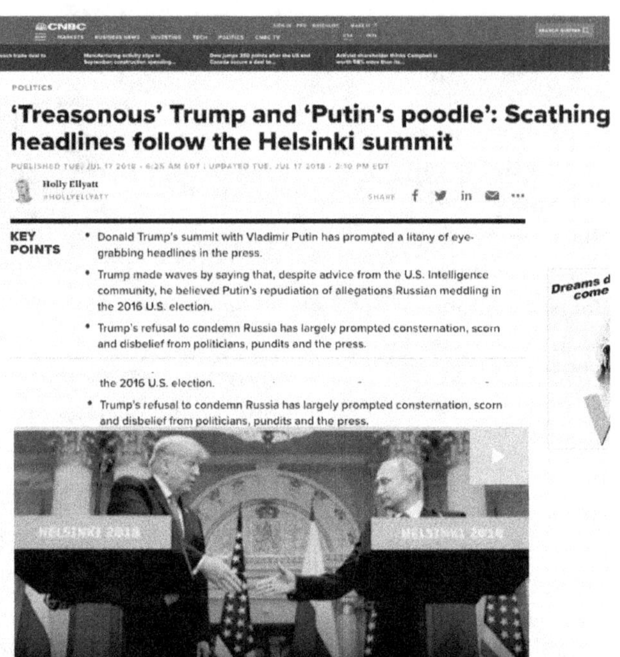

'Treasonous' Trump and 'Putin's poodle': Scathing headlines follow the Helsinki summit

occurred on British soil—to paint Donald Trump as a dupe of President Putin and Russia.

The second stage also occurred during the campaign, from roughly July 2016, when a completely unprecedented and legally ungrounded FBI counterintelligence investigation was opened on the Presidential nominee of a major political party. This stage involved the unleashing of the hoax that the Democratic National Committee had been hacked by the Russians through the November 2016 election. This stage also was completely reliant on the British, including GCHQ, and the dirty dossier authored and weaponized by former MI6 Russia desk chief Christopher Steele. Steele's allegations were given credence for purposes of the British information warfare operation against Trump, by the fact that the dirty unverified Steele dossier was being investigated by the FBI.

This stage involved an all-out effort to defeat the Trump candidacy using every tool of British intelligence, with funding by the Clinton campaign and direction from Obama and the White House, all of which focused again on the fake account of Trump's ties to Russia and his compromise by prostitutes there, coupled with claims that Russia was stealing information about Clinton via hacking and handing it to Trump.

Finally, there was the stage which went from roughly November 2016 through Comey's firing

CC/Rich Girard

Former FBI Director James Comey.

in May, an all-out effort to dismantle the Trump presidency and, by blackmail, tame the President away from his vow to end perpetual warfare on this planet and establish sane relationships with Russia and China, a vow which threatens the British Empire existentially.

Comey has already testified to numerous efforts to set the President up for charges of obstruction of justice, conducting "murder boards" at the Justice Department with his close friends throughout his contacts with the President, writing endless memos about these contacts, and engaging in a "J. Edgar Hoover moment" when he confronted the President with the dirty British MI6 product called the Christopher Steele dossier.

Rod Rosenstein went to the White House on September 21 to urge the President to hold off from immediate declassification of key coup documents based on objections from Britain and Australia. The President agreed to have Michael Horowitz, the Department of Justice Inspector General, review the documents, but stated that he expected that review to be expedited, and that speed was very important to him.

In an interview on WMAL radio September 24, former U.S. Attorney for the District of Columbia, Joseph DiGenova said, "The UK is at the center of a conspiracy to frame Donald Trump and Carter Page, and George Papadopoulos. This is all about [Joseph] Mifsud, and protecting [Stefan] Halper, and Alexander Downer. Downer is a big fish. And all of the work that all of them did with GCHQ.... This is a huge, huge problem for the UK. They may ultimately say, 'Look, you can talk about Steele, but please don't talk about Alexander Downer.' They are very worried about the role that Downer played in this."

Pat Buchanan noted yesterday that the integrity of the American Republic is far more important than the embarrassment of the British in this affair. Buchanan cited a *Wall Street Journal* piece to the same effect.

3. There is a sitting grand jury in Washington, D.C. which has begun to hear evidence about the crimes implicit in the coup against Donald Trump. The initial focus is on former Deputy FBI Director Andrew McCabe, who is under investigation for lying about media leaks. McCabe's memos are the source of the *New York Times* leak about Rosenstein's perfidies. It is clear that McCabe is intent on bringing down his co-conspirators and those he thinks hung him out to dry, in order to save himself.

The remedies lie, as Alan Dershowitz has said, in getting everyone involved in the May 2017 meetings involving Rosenstein, under oath about what happened there, and doing so, in whatever forum, urgently and quickly. A first step in that direction was announced by Republicans in the House of Representatives yesterday. They have secured Rosenstein's appearance to testify before them about the May meetings, and they have also subpoenaed Andrew McCabe's notes on these meetings, which were the source of the *New York Times* story.

In addition, Rosenstein is scheduled to discuss those May meetings with the President some time this next week. Presumably, in this context, the President is not going to sit still concerning Justice Department delay of his declassification order of the documents now being reviewed by the Inspector General.

This brings me to the elections and what you can do about all of this.

There's something I'm going to repeat like a mantra, and invite you to really discuss here. It's simple: Turn out and vote and get others to do so! Demand that the candidates endorse LaRouche PAC's "Campaign to Secure the Future." Organize the major supporters of those candidates to do the same. Build, through these elections, a political movement based on these principles. But, as they often say on late night television, there is more—something which you urgently need to consider as you organize for this.

Making America Great Again: the Missing Ingredient

In March 2017 I wrote a major article for *Executive Intelligence Review* documenting the British role in the coup against the President, with the subhead, "Who Really is George Soros, Anyway?" In that article I said that to defeat the coup, we Americans need to learn our own revolutionary history, which has been suppressed, particularly the principles of the Public Credit System enunciated by Alexander Hamilton and the modern scientific enrichment of those principles as developed by Lyndon LaRouche over the last forty-five years.

These are the proven principles which have served

America for more than two centuries. These ideas drove the sustained economic and scientific progress found in Hamilton's early United States, during the Abraham Lincoln Administration, and during the recovery and World War II mobilization led by Franklin Roosevelt. They were fundamentally advanced by LaRouche's breakthrough discoveries providing the scientific metrics for sustained economic and social progress. They are encapsulated in LaRouche's "Four New Laws to Save the USA Now."

I also cited two glaring vulnerabilities of the decadent post-World War II "New World Order" created by the British and their American friends after Franklin Roosevelt's death.

The chief vulnerability of that Order is its complete disregard for the fundamental laws of physical economic science. Addicted to monetary gambling, it simply does not know how to build an economy capable of sustained social and economic progress. It banks its survival on continued enslavement of subject populations through propaganda, dumbed-down education, entertainment, drugs, and perpetual wars. Like Rome—the imperial model for this modern day British Empire—it is doomed to fail. The issue is whether the entire human race vanishes with it in a nuclear catastrophe.

The second vulnerability is found in the criminal, anti-human history of the New World Order itself. If this is understood fully, if the smoke-and-mirrors magic show stops, the British are doomed.

In 1956, after Stalin had died, amidst challenges from Third World countries seeking economic development, and foreseeing the emergence of a new generation on the horizon, Congress for Cultural Freedom (CCF) sociologist Daniel Bell took leave from his post as labor editor of Henry Luce's *Fortune* magazine to become the director of CCF's Seminar Planning Committee. In April 1957, the first seminar was held in Tokyo, entitled, "Problems of Economic Growth." According to British journalist and historian, Frances Stonor Saunders, "The [CCF] Conference was the pre-

Bookforum.com
Congress for Cultural Freedom sociologist Daniel Bell.

cursor of the impending shift by development economists from an emphasis on *growth of per capita income to one of the quality of social justice and freedom as the true measure of development*." Bell would later author *The Coming of Post-Industrial Society*, formally ushering in the so-called consumer and information society.

One might add a final irony concerning the Kavanaugh matter. Here you are, in a society in which pornography has become the most popular entertainment, an ascendancy which has gone on and on unchecked, protected by the so-called sexual revolution which made women the equal of males in all forms of debauchery—what is called "social freedom." The Democratic Party senators, who, it could be very readily shown, were largely complicit in flooding our country with this junk, now stand firm against a Catholic who they allege drank too much in high school, seeking to tar and feather him.

The Post-Industrial Society

The New Left and the counter-culture which emerged in the 1960s were the synthetic ideological products of this shift.

Not surprisingly, workers who still identified with economic progress, the nation state, and the legacy of Franklin Roosevelt, became primary targets of New Left students. They were castigated for their psychologically "repressed" and "backward" identities. Teachers, white and black, inclined to emphasize universal values, became the targets of black activists demanding "community control" of schools.

As Lyndon LaRouche emphasized in founding documents of his organization, these "new left" ideas were drawn from the syndicalism of Benito Mussolini's fascist state and the national bolshevism of Gregor Strasser, ideas identical with what FDR's intelligence services labeled, "Synarchism/Nazi-Communist." Their "community control" social structures were derived directly from the Tavistock Institute's Kurt Lewin and his studies of the dynamics of small groups. Their smallness precludes attempts to exert major influence on

Zbigniew Brzezinski

actual existential issues. Setting numerous such groups into competitive contiguity, where gains by one group are at the expense of another, creates the basis for a self-policing fascist order. Atomize the subject population, set race against race, language group against language group, women against men, etc.—and then mobilize these groups together against mass political and trade union organizations, all under the banner of anti-authoritarianism and local community control. There you have fascism with a democratic face.

Similarly, the "environmentalism" so central to the counterculture, was a critical idea in Adolph Hitler's Malthusian arsenal—oneness with an overpowering and arbitrary nature that man's reason has repeatedly and criminally violated, in an illegitimate search for non-existent scientific truth. Prince Philip, who has wished to be reincarnated as a virus capable of wiping out whole swaths of humanity in order to control population, has been demonstrated to be the intellectual godfather of this movement.[1]

Thus the post-industrial consumer and service-economy society emerged from a generation which had been psychologically "shocked" repeatedly by the assassinations of President John Kennedy, Martin Luther King, and Robert Kennedy, all potential

advocates for advancing Roosevelt's vision. The nation was mired for years in the senseless genocide of the war in Viet Nam, creating a cultural pessimism which persists to this day. Widespread use of drugs, sexual hedonism, and blaring, atonal Rock music produced mental oblivion in large swaths of the American population.

The revelations that the entirety of post-war American culture was one intelligence community-manufactured mess should have sparked a popular revolt, to return America to its republican roots in the Constitution's model of an educated and engaged citizenry, through its representative institutions, deliberating national and international issues. Instead, as a result of the counterculture, featuring the likes of Herbert Marcuse and others, these revelations became the cynical rationale for the edict: "tune in, turn on, drop out."

In May 1975, the David Rockefeller-dominated Trilateral Commission issued a report entitled *The Crisis of Democracy* at a conference in Kyoto, Japan. The report, authored by Samuel Huntington, Michel Crozier, and Joji Watanuki, under Zbiginiew Brzezinski's direction, recognized that the Anglo-Americans faced a governance problem in the transition to a post-

U.S. combat operations at Ia Drang Valley, Vietnam, November 1965.

industrial society.

The collapse of the Bretton Woods system in 1971 (presaged by the 1965-67 recessions), resulted in a decade in which Wall Street's elite were only barely able to hold off total economic collapse through the oil shocks of the 70s and the savage wage and price austerity measures imposed by the Nixon Administration. At

---

1. See, e.g., "The Coming Fall of the House of Windsor," *EIR*, October 28, 1994.

the same time, third world nations were calling for real development of their economies in a new just economic order that would turn their economies from colonial raw material satrapies into modern nation states. Lyndon and Helga La-Rouche played an extremely significant role leading this fight, setting forth an agenda of great projects, debt moratoria, and an International Development Bank.[2]

Huntington warned about a "democratic surge" afflicting the United States and other nations. Too many people wanting too many things from government—and, ultimately, too much participation in government—was making governance too difficult. Expectations had to be thwarted, and new counterinsurgency institutions needed to be forged. The crisis demanded corporatist solutions, through what one Trilateral apologist openly called "fascism with a democratic face." One of the key proposals was a new institute for the "cooperative promotion of democracy." This proposal would come to fruition under Ronald Reagan in the form of the National Endowment for Democracy.

In lockstep with these developments, in 1975 the Council on Foreign Relations (CFR), headquartered in New York City, embarked on a set of studies to modernize the forms of the Anglo-American Empire—the "1980s Project" prospectus of the CFR. The studies were also overseen by Brzezinski and future cabinet members of the Carter Administration, including Cyrus Vance, Leslie Gelb, Richard Cooper, Marshall D. Shulman, and W. Michael Blumenthal. The focus of this project was countering the "Hamiltonian" pro-development perspective and demands of the developing world. The CFR proposed "controlled disintegration" of the world's industrial economies, ruralization and destruction of cities in the developing sector, and a strategic approach to Russia which would force it to limit the growth of science and technology or face general thermonuclear war. It proposed to develop and police a

Samuel Huntington

series of alternate paths, or "critical choices," for arriving at the specified objectives. The mandate of Anglo-American foreign policy was to compel other nations to choose among these pre-selected alternate paths. The fact that the nations got to choose their own path to self-destruction constituted "democracy."

The most succinct presentation of the CFR's concerns was that of Fred Hirsch, editor of the London *Economist*, in his book, *Alternatives to Monetary Disorder* (1977). In that book for the 1980s Project, Hirsch asserts that the central conflict in economic theory is between the American System (Alexander Hamilton, Friedrich List, et al.) and the British liberal system (Adam Smith, David Ricardo, et al.), and he ascribes the developing world's demand for a new economic order to the taint of the "mercantilist" American System. He claims that Russia and China also suffer from this American taint in their development proposals. He attacks Hamilton and List by name.

EIR rightly labeled the incompetence inherent in "controlled disintegration" of the world's economy as "A Conspiracy of Morons" at the time.[3] However, these morons were also murderers, bent on the genocidal goal of reducing the world's population through famines, wars, or by whatever means. That policy had already been formalized by Henry Kissinger in National Security Study Memorandum 200 (1974).

In the meantime, under the Trilateral Commission-sponsored Presidency of Jimmy Carter, Wall Street's Paul Volcker continued the relentless war on U.S. living standards through the high interest rate policies he set as Chairman of the Federal Reserve Bank. Working Democrats and farmers, decimated by this economic warfare and faced with a Democratic Platform which embraced the cultural priorities of the New Left, began leaving the Democratic Party in droves. The British and their Trilateral friends went to work building a new homogenous political culture, which featured an anti-Soviet Democratic Party occupying the left and center,

<hr>

2. See Matthew Ogden, "A Forty Year Fight for a New Economic Order," *EIR*, October 24, 2014.

3. "A Conspiracy of Morons," *EIR*, May 15, 1979.

and an anti-Soviet conservative and neo-conservative Republican Party on the right. Each would endorse the free market, post-industrial society nostrums of Wall Street, and counter-insurgency operations against pro-Soviet, nationalist or neutral regimes.

It was under these auspices that the huge outsourcing of American manufacturing jobs to China was undertaken. It also had a geopolitical component. China was sold advanced U.S. technologies and defense technologies on the theory that China would act as a chess piece in America's war on the Soviet Union. One of the authors of this geopolitical strategy, in addition to Henry Kissinger, was Michael Pillsbury.

In his United Nations speech this week, President Trump blew up this entire post-war order. He declared, as he had before, that America was returning to the foreign policies wisely enunciated by John Quincy Adams. We would no longer engage in regime-change wars. We view the world not through globalist institutions, but through developing relations between sovereign nation states. Both implicit and enunciated in his speech was the idea that every nation and every people is entitled to what Lyndon LaRouche would call a "full set" economy, rather than outsourcing supply chains and jobs under the rubric of British-designed "free trade." This speech was a very big deal. But the transformation is, as with everything with Trump, incomplete. It is, after all, a transformation in which our enemies still hold substantial bases of power.

When Donald Trump came into office, he had, unexpectedly, to assemble a government—and the only wheels around were the decadent shards of the extant Republican Party. That is why you often see the President saying one thing, which appears revolutionary, and his entire government appearing to move in the opposite direction, based on the old order the President repeatedly says he wants to blow up. Most recently, the

voachinese.com/Li Yihua

Michael Pillsbury

old guard has focused on ramping up tensions between the United States and Russia, and the United States and China.

It is these traitors, really, who should be our biggest targets. If each nation in the world is entitled to a "full set" economy, that can't happen under the present, post-1971 monetary regime emanating from Wall Street and the City of London. There is no escaping this fact. If Russia, China, and other nations attempt to survive the hideous regime of sanctions—imposed by the current wild Congress and Obama ringers left over in the Trump Administration—by developing alternative currency arrangements, without attacking the center of the evil, they will, at this point, probably bring the world to the edge of war.

The alternative to this is exactly the one Lyndon LaRouche has proposed: Take the strongest and most populous economies of the world—Russia, China, India, and the United States—and have them sit down together to set up a new monetary system—cancelling the unpayable debts and fictitious financial paper, and creating a credit institution that will fund worldwide development—not horizontally, in the present modes of technology, but going for breakthroughs like fusion power, which can take the human race to the next level of development. Start with President Trump, President Putin, President Xi, and Prime Minister Modi discussing this topic, one on one, and together.

Which brings me to Michael Pillsbury. President Trump mentioned him last week at the UN as a key advisor on China, and Vice-President Pence praises him to the skies. Pillsbury claims, falsely, that China is on a long march to become the world's new hegemon and is playing the West for suckers. He demands an all-out confrontation and a substantial scaling back of the Belt and Road. He is really the major saboteur, right now, of our march to a new just economic order and the ending of wars. We have a lot of work to do on him but I'll just give you his basic biographical outline. This is what he says about himself online:

> [Quoting Raymond Garthoff:] "Michael Pillsbury first floated the idea of arms sales and broad range of American military security relationships with China in a much-discussed article in *Foreign Policy* in the fall of 1975. Not known then was that Pillsbury had been conducting secret talks with Chinese officials.... [H]is reports were circulated to a dozen or so top officials of the NSC, Department of Defense and Department of State as secret documents."

> [According to an article in the book, *U.S.-China Cold War Collaboration, 1971-1989*, by S. Mahmud Ali:] "The man spearheading the effort was not a public official, and enjoyed deniability. Michael Pillsbury, a China analyst at the RAND Corporation ... spent the summer of 1973 secretly meeting PLA officers stationed under diplomatic cover at China's UN mission.... The DoD managed Pillsbury. Pillsbury filed a report, L-32, in March 1974.... L-32 was a seminal paper on which subsequent US-PRC military cooperation blossomed."

Journalist James Mann wrote,

> Outward appearances indicate that Pillsbury may have been working with American intelligence agencies from the very start of his relationship with General Zhang.... In the fall of 1973, Pillsbury submitted a classified memo suggesting the novel idea that the United States might establish a military relationship with China.... This was the genesis of the idea of a 'China card,' the notion that the United States might use China to gain Cold War advantage over the Soviet Union. The idea would eventually come to dominate American thinking about the new relationship with China.

Pillsbury participated in President Reagan's decision in 1986 to order the CIA to arm the Afghan resistance with Stinger missiles. According to the UN Undersecretary General who negotiated the Soviet withdrawal from Afghanistan, "Initially, the Stinger campaign was spearheaded by Undersecretary of Defense for Policy Fred Iklé and his aggressive Coordinator for Afghan Affairs, Michael Pillsbury.... The Stinger proponents won their victory in the face of overwhelming bureaucratic resistance that persisted until the very end of the struggle." Mann wrote, "For Michael Pillsbury, the covert operations in Afghanistan represented the fulfillment of the decade-old dream of American military cooperation with China ... To help him win the argument, Pillsbury made use of his China connections."

George Crile stated in the 2007 film drama, *Charlie Wilson's War*, that "Ironically, neither [Gust] Avrakotos nor [Charlie] Wilson was directly involved in the decision and claims any credit."

Among the people that most say were supplied with these weapons was Osama Bin Laden, although Pillsbury is at pains to distance himself from this.

Pillsbury also played a leading role in the founding of the Institute for Peace and the National Endowment for Democracy, both critical components in the regime-change wars that Donald Trump has condemned.

Conclusion: An architect of the outsourcing of U.S. jobs and technology, not on behalf of China, but on behalf of British geopolitical goals; an architect of the Afghan war and the sale of U.S military technology to terrorists; an architect of the key institutions for conducting disastrous regime-change operations throughout the world.

I'll end with the words of my friend, the poet, Percy Bysshe Shelley. As you look back upon the last week and its attack on our Republic, take back that wonder and *hope*—now armed with a future vision and an educated serenity, ready to laugh at those you thought could drive you to rage and impotent cynicism by their slaughter, last week, of the bedrock values we hold dear:

> "And that slaughter to the Nation
> Shall steam up like inspiration,
> Eloquent, oracular;
> A volcano heard afar.
>
> "And these words shall then become
> Like Oppression's thundered doom
> Ringing through each heart and brain,
> Heard again—again—again—
>
> "Rise like Lions after slumber
> In unvanquishable number—
> Shake your chains to earth like dew
> Which in sleep had fallen on you—
> Ye are many—they are few."

Discredited Russiagate Coup Must Be Shut Down For the Sake of Humanity

This is an edited transcript of the Schiller Institute's Sept. 27, 2018 New Paradigm interview with Helga Zepp-LaRouche, by Harley Schlanger. A video of the webcast is available.

Harley Schlanger: Hello, I'm Harley Schlanger welcoming you to this week's webcast of the Schiller Institute, our weekly international strategic discussion with Helga Zepp-LaRouche, founder of the Schiller Institutes. There's an extraordinary series of developments around the meeting of the UN General Assembly. I think it's very important that people get a sense of what's occurring and what the implications are. In this webcast, we're also going to take a look at the fallout from the declassification order from President Trump, what's going on with Rod Rosenstein and his role.

I think the best place to start is Trump's speech to the United Nations General Assembly. Helga, how did you see the speech—its importance, the pros and cons?

Trump's Speech at the UN

Helga Zepp-LaRouche: The European/Western mainstream media chose to only report that Trump got laughter after he praised the accomplishments of his administration, and they blocked out entirely what were the really important aspects of his speech *and* the many bilateral diplomatic activities. You have to take all of this

as one picture to really understand what is going on, as you say. On the one hand, the coup attempt against Trump is still ongoing; on the other hand it's clear that this may be defeated in a relatively short period of time. So the situation is really dramatic.

I think the strong points of Trump's speech were clearly that he emphasized the right and need of having sovereignty for every country. He praised other cultures as being extremely important. He made a very articulated pledge for patriotism, which was quite different from the flat, two-dimensional pitch of people like Steve Bannon, but was actually important and very good.

White House/Joyce N. Boghosian

President Trump addressing the 73rd session of the UN General Assembly, UN Headquarters, New York, Sept. 25, 2018.

Trump attacked the failure of the free trade institutions, the failure of the World Trade Organization, and the International Criminal Court, and the Human Rights Council of the United Nations—all institutions which we have criticized for very similar reasons.

So I think the speech overall was very important.

There were some problematic points in it, which I will go into in a second. But I think one has to first look at the total spectrum of diplomatic activities that Trump conducted on the sidelines. First of all, he met with President Moon Jae-in from South Korea. This was quite remarkable, because it highlights what we had characterized as the potential for a "Singapore model," following the summit of Trump with North Korea's leader Kim Jong-un last July. At that time I said that the "Singapore model" can be applied to *every* crisis in the world. For example, in the spirit of the New Silk Road, by changing just a few parameters, the crisis between North and South Korea, and between North Korea and the United States, turned from confrontation into win-win cooperation, which is now possible because of the environment of the Belt and Road Initiative.

Contrary to the press reports, this diplomacy *is* working. I would like Western so-called leaders to just reflect on the fact that President Moon Jae-in of South Korea said on September 25, that Trump has become more than a friend, that he has telephoned him twenty times, had seven summits, and that they have complete and perfect trust. I think Russian Foreign Minister

President Trump: Every country has a right and need of sovereignty. UNGA, Sept. 25, 2018.

Sergey Lavrov commented on the success of Trump in the North Korea developments, pledging that Russia, for its part, would do everything possible for the economic development of North Korea, including the development of infrastructure. It is being mooted that Trump will meet with Kim Jong-un fairly soon, so this is all on a very good track.

So I think this is the big success story of the Trump Administration, which is completely blacked out by the mainstream media.

Trump also had a sideline summit with Prime Minister Shinzo Abe of Japan, another extremely important development, this time, not so much between Japan and the United States, but between Japan and Russia, because what Abe said in his UN General Assembly speech, was that he hopes to have a peace treaty with Russia before the end of the year. And I should have also mentioned that North and South Korea pledged a peace treaty, also before the end of the year, and unification.

Back to Japan: Abe said that if such a

President Trump meets with Moon Jae-in, President of the Republic of Korea on the sidelines of the UNGA. New York Palace Hotel, New York City, Sept. 24, 2018.

White House/Shealah Craighead

President Trump meets with Israeli Prime Minister Benjamin Netanyahu on the sidelines of the UNGA. UN Headquarters, New York, Sept. 26, 2018.

peace treaty between Japan and Russia is signed, it will contribute greatly to peace and stability in the entire East Asia region.

So here you have two extremely important strategic developments, which are almost not mentioned in the mainstream media.

While President Trump really attacked Iran, it's not Iran, in my view, which is entirely responsible for terrorism. Look at what Saudi Arabia is still doing in Yemen. One should have a more balanced view. One can only hope that President Trump is preparing a Middle East general peace plan. There are indications that he's doing that. For example, Trump also met with Israeli Prime Minister Benjamin Netanyahu, and after that said that he would endorse a two-state solution between Israel and Palestine,

White House.Shealah Craighead

President Trump meets with Japanese Prime Minister Shinzo Abe on the sidelines of the UNGA, Trump Tower, New York City, Sept. 23, 2018.

that it would be left up them, if they wanted to have a one-state or a two-state solution, but it is very important that he reiterated the endorsement for a two-state solution. Obviously, this is very difficult, after all the illegal settlements that have been built in recent years—but nevertheless, this is also on the way.

And one sign that there may be actually a broader, more strategic plan underway, is that President Trump also met with the new Italian Prime Minister, Giuseppe Conte, on the sidelines of the UN General Assembly, and there they discussed not only Libya, the whole Mediterranean policy, but according to some Italian press reports, they also discussed the possibility of Italy playing a mediating role between the United States and Iran. Now this is very important, because Italy is the only Western country that has developed a positive attitude of cooperation with the Trump Administration. This was visible at the G7 meeting in Canada. Conte has already visited the White House, and now they have continued that cooperation. I think this is very, very important, because Italy not only works with President Trump, but as the recent trips of the different Italian ministers and cabinet members to China demonstrate, Italy is the one European country which has developed excellent relations with China, and China is obviously important in the background of the Iran question.

As you can see, this is a very widespread and complicated network of diplomatic activities, which is being carried out very skillfully, completely counter to the way in which at least the European media and naturally the mainstream media in the United States are characterizing Trump, and the evil accusations of coup plotters, that he is a misfit and is not capable of handling things. In the context of the UN General Assembly, Trump is portraying quite the opposite—a very far-sighted diplomatic effort involving many parts of the world and many crisis spots.

This is all very interesting, and we should look at these things in a differentiated, new, and not black-and-white way in which you are either for Trump or against Trump. As we have said many times, the relationships of the United States, Russia, and China are really the essence of the ability to maintain peace, and therefore everything which has to do with that is of the utmost importance.

China: Return to Principles of Westphalia

Schlanger: Trump's discussion of sovereignty, not forcing our so-called "values" on other countries, was welcomed by some of the people—Lavrov. The Chinese commented on it. But there was also a back-and-forth between Trump and Chinese officials, the Chinese media. I'd like to hear your comments on that.

Zepp-LaRouche: Well, the Chinese Foreign Minister Wang Yi met with American and Chinese businessmen in the context of this UN General Assembly, and he reiterated the absolute necessity of going back to a positive U.S.-China relationship. So from the Chinese side, from the official government level, they keep emphasizing the need to have a positive relationship. Wang Yi naturally reacted very sharply and quickly to the accusation of Trump that the Chinese had meddled in the midterm election—this seems to refer to a four-page insert in the *Des Moines Register* paid for by *China Daily*, which said that Trump's tariff-based trade policies would hurt Iowan soybean farmers, making it harder for them to export to China.

I don't know if that's "meddling" or not. In any case, on a lower level, namely the media level, the Chinese have made the point that at stake with these trade issues, is not just tit-for-tat tariffs, not just the U.S. sale of weapons to Taiwan, violating the one-China policy, not the sanctions against China because China bought some weapons systems from Russia; but as one insightful article in the *Global Times* says, "That the issue is increasingly moving beyond trade, is the real cause of concern, and that is where the real danger lies. The con-

sequences become hard to predict. That is why signs of accelerating strain on mutual goodwill deserve serious attention from both parties." I think that is really what's at stake.

So I really wish that President Trump would return to where he started with President Xi Jinping at Mar-a-Lago and then the state-plus visit in Beijing at the end of last year, because too much is at stake. Anyway, I just think there needs to be a change in the policy.

Russian Foreign Ministry spokeswoman Maria Zakharova said, it's very good that Trump talks about sovereignty, but this should apply to all countries, not just the United States. And another comment in the Chinese media was similar, saying the same thing: that sovereignty is very good, but equality is equally

Xinhua/Wang Ying

Chinese State Councilor and Foreign Minister Wang Yi (5th from left) meets with representatives from the National Committee on U.S.-China Relations and the U.S.-China Business Council, New York City, Sept. 24, 2018.

important, and both are values that came out of—interesting for the Chinese to say—out of the Peace of Westphalia, and we must return to the principles of the Peace of Westphalia, which was exactly sovereignty, equality, policy in the interest of the other, and even love in foreign policy, and the role of the state in the reconstruction of a country after the war: These are all important principles of the Peace of Westphalia, and it is quite right to say that we must urgently return to them.

Schlanger: People want to know what you think Trump was talking about when he attacked the International Criminal Court (ICC), and said that it was good that the United States had pulled out of it. What is the ICC, and what's the importance of Trump's attack?

Zepp-LaRouche: The ICC is basically an international court which in the past has been extremely biased. It has only gone after African leaders; it has taken a very biased position in the legal suit of previous Philippine governments against China concerning the South China Sea. So I think it is indeed a very dubious court, and it was quite good that Trump attacked it.

1980s Project for Controlled Disintegration

Schlanger: What about Trump's talking up the great success of his economic policies? One of his real weaknesses—one which you have pointed out repeatedly, and one that we've covered in our publications—is that he's making the same mistake that was made before, of looking at the stock market as some kind of measure of economic success. This could be a very serious problem, couldn't it?

Zepp-LaRouche: I want to read to you some recent figures. There are many people pointing to the potential for an immediate financial blowout, to occur even before the midterm elections. All the figures are really warning signs: state debt as of 2018, compared to 2008, is 104% higher; consumer debt, 44.7% higher; student debt, 165.3% higher; corporate debt, 72.7% higher.

Trump has said that the U.S. trade deficit with China occurred after China joined the World Trade Organization (WTO). Now that's not exactly what happened, because China joined the WTO in 2001, but as we have pointed out, and especially as my husband Lyndon LaRouche has stated in the context of his Presidential campaigns, in numerous speeches, articles, and TV addresses, the reason why the United States went the wrong way has everything to do with the paradigm shift which occurred in 1960s.

EIRNS

Lyndon LaRouche campaigning for President at a Westinghouse plant in Philadelphia, PA, 1976.

Blown up blast furnace of U.S. Steel Corp. in McKeesport, PA.

McKeesport Daily News

I remember very well him campaigning against this very clearly in the 1976 Presidential campaign, because at that point, you had the New York Council on Foreign Relations and the Trilateral Commission initiating what they called the 1980s Project, a call for "controlled disintegration" of the U.S. and Western economy, proposing to move from an industrial society into a post-industrial society. They did various studies which were published by McGraw-Hill—I think altogether over 30 books, covering every aspect of the planet, how this "controlled disintegration" should work. Among other things, the 1980s Project was a projection of artificially induced shocks, such as an interest rate increase, an energy price increase, the cut-off of credit, and similar means of manipulation. Its idea of deindustrialization, or post-industrial society, went along with the idea of outsourcing "unwanted" industries to cheap-labor countries.

This corresponded to the initial phase of China's opening up, where China made itself a cheap-labor

Austrian Chancellor Sebastian Kurz.

market, but this was not pushed, at least not alone by China. It was pushed by the Carter Administration, by the New York Council on Foreign Relations, by the Trilateral Commission, as it was by the World Wildlife Fund and the Club of Rome. All these institutions expressed different aspects of this paradigm shift. And it led to mistakes on the part of China, such as not respecting the environment, just going for cheap labor production, which the Chinese government has long ago recognized and is moving very hard to remedy, such as making extremely important efforts to clean the air, to clean the groundwater, and other effects of its earlier policy.

The reason Detroit and the other rust belt cities are deindustrialized has a lot to do with these policies. Pittsburgh, for example, is a case study in such deindustrialization as is, by the way, North Rhine-Westphalia, the former industrial heartland of Germany, now almost worse off than many of the former East German states.

Obviously, the WTO is also a problem, but I think you have to look much deeper if you want to correct this policy and reindustrialize, but reindustrialize with the most modern technologies, such as fusion and space technologies in win-win cooperation in the context of the Belt and Road Initiative. There needs to be a real discussion: Go back to the American System of economy, which Trump in various rallies said he absolutely admires and praised.

We need a correction to Trump's vision, because I think one of the Achilles' heels, if not *the* Achilles' heel of the Trump Administration, is the danger of a financial blowout, which could occur at any moment. If we really want to get to the root of the problem we must go back to those paradigm shifts, starting in the 1960s and the 1970s, whose aim was to replace modern industrial cities with post-industrial "utopias."

Breakup of the EU Just a Matter of Time

Schlanger: I think you would argue that part of the effect of the postindustrial policy has been to create an overall economy which makes governments completely incapable of governing. We see this throughout Europe now. We were talking earlier about Germany. It's probably just a matter of time before something breaks up the EU, before the Merkel government in Germany collapses. Where do things stand right now in Europe, Helga?

Zepp-LaRouche: The German situation is terrible, because of what has been played out in the case of Hans-Georg Maassen, the head of the BfV, the equivalent of the FBI in Germany. Maassen made some really incompetent remarks concerning a video—a fake video—covering the right-wing demonstrations following a murder in Chemnitz. This led to a deal between the SPD and CDU and CSU, to kick Maassen upstairs to Undersecretary in the Interior Ministry, at a higher pay grade, which naturally upset a lot of people. So then, SPD head Andrea Nahles responded and said, No, we have to renegotiate it.

I don't want to go through the details—because for an international audience this is probably confusing—but what it showed very clearly to Germans is that these government representatives do not care about the future of Germany, they don't care about the common good; they only care about their own posts, their own power position. And naturally, the CDU and CSU and SPD are falling in the polls like a rock.

Now the danger in all of this is that the right-wing Alternative for Germany party (AfD), which is no alternative at all because it has absolutely no solutions, is now in the polls the second most numerous party, which is really a big problem and reminds you of the 1930s. Even so, one cannot totally equate this with the 1930s, but in that party, you have some really hard-core evil people.

This leaves a situation where everybody is speculating on when Merkel will be out. Today the big tabloid daily *Bildzeitung* has a banner headline, "Who Will Write the Letter to Her?" referring to the fact it was Angela Merkel who brought about the fall of fellow CDUer, Chancellor Helmut Kohl, in 1999, by writing an open letter to him, which was quite an act of disloyalty. So basically *Bildzeitung* is now calling for a rebellion against her, as she has just lost the vote for faction leader in the Bundestag. And the CDU's partner, the Bavarian Party, CSU, which has an election coming up on October 14, is also dropping in the polls like a stone.

So this does not look good, because if we have new elections in Germany—if there is not a complete change in the policy—it could not lead to any better result than the further rise of the AfD.

Then there is the European Union (EU). You know, many people say, just one shot and the European Union may fall apart. There are now several large EU member states—Italy, Spain and France—that no longer respect the budget discipline imposed by the EU Commission. The whole thing is in disarray, and the only two countries with any positive orientation at all are Italy, because of its relationship to China and also to Trump, and Austria, where Chancellor Sebastian Kurz is organizing a major European-African forum before the end of the year.

So, you have a completely disunified European Union, but you have some promising anomalies. But what's happening in the larger picture is definitely not taking place in Europe right now, except for what I said about Italy and Austria.

Schlanger: To come back to the United States, one of the things you mentioned is that the effect of the mass media not covering what Trump is actually saying and doing, is directly related to Russiagate. That there's been a complete change in the last months of the coverage, I think, is in large part due to what we've done in showing the importance of the British role—using Christopher Steele, using these various sting operations with Joseph Mifsud and Stefan Halper, Alexander Downer. And now we see on the firing line, Deputy Attorney General Rod Rosenstein. This new coverage is crucial, because if Trump will follow through, as he said he would, with the declassification, the documents can put into the public discussion the fact that all of Russiagate from the beginning was designed to stop Trump from moving the United States into the new paradigm.

Can you summarize for us where things stand now regarding Rod Rosenstein, and the fight to blow apart the fraudulent "narrative" of Russiagate?

Declassify the Documents!

Zepp-LaRouche: Well, today Trump and Rosenstein are supposed to meet. We have to see what comes of that. But the background is that there are now increasing signs that in May 2017 there was a meeting in which Rosenstein participated with high-level Department of Justice and FBI officials. At that meeting there was a discussion of using the 25th Amendment to the Constitution to get Trump out of the White House, and in order to develop evidence for that, to have Rod Rosenstein wear a wire to secretly record Trump.

That was leaked by the *New York Times* a week ago, and Rosenstein immediately denied everything. But the point is, if he did participate in such a highly treasonous meeting and did not blow the whistle right away, which he obviously didn't, but instead, he appointed Robert Mueller as a Special Counsel for an unprecedented investigation against a sitting American President, based on a complete web of false dossiers, and orchestrations and so forth. Rosenstein obviously felt that after the leak of the *New York Times*, he could not testify in the Congress, so he offered his resignation to White House Chief of Staff John Kelly. So we'll have to see.

The demand made by civil liberties lawyer Alan Dershowitz, as the only way to solve this, is that everything concerning the May 2017 meeting be immediately made public. Those present have to be asked under oath what happened. And everything concerning the role of the British must be published also. There are now more and more people who are aware that this is a coup. For example, Sen. Lindsey Graham said this is a "bureaucratic coup" in action.

And yes, Rosenstein went to the White House in the meantime and said that the declassification should be delayed, because the British and the Australian governments objected. Other people have said the whole "Five Eyes" intelligence relationship will be blown, the British-American "special relationship" will be blown. If that happens it would be a good thing, not a bad thing!

CC/Internet Education Foundation

Deputy Attorney General Rod Rosenstein.

So, all the documents should be declassified immediately, because, as Pat Buchanan correctly said, the integrity of the American republic is more important than an embarrassment for the British.

I think this is really a countdown. Because of the British and the Australian complaints, President Trump put Michael Horowitz, the Inspector General of the Department of Justice, in charge of reviewing all of the documents. Trump encouraged Horowitz to follow through with absolute speed, because speed was of the utmost essence in this, and that is absolutely true.

But what is at stake here, just to reiterate, is an absolutely unprecedented meddling, not by Russia, but by the British government, by the GCHQ, by the British Secret Intelligence Service MI6, and that must be put out in the open, because that is the way the British Empire is maneuvering, and that must be absolutely stopped if the world is to live in peace.

Do Not Sit on the Sidelines!

We are in an absolutely fascinating situation, and I would urge all of you not to sit on the sidelines, on the fence, because this is a period when history is being made. Trump is doing extremely important things, and if he is not correct on all points, that is not the point. When has a President *ever* attacked those institutions of the British Empire?

I think this is very important, so we should really understand that the midterm election is important for war and peace, and if some things are not right, don't focus on those things, focus on what is really essential. Help us to bring in the economic discussion, of the physical science of economy as it was developed by Lyndon LaRouche, help us to bring others to see the utmost importance of convening a New Bretton Woods conference, immediately, among the most important powers—United States, Russia, China, and India. This is the focus of our mobilization both in Washington, and also in the UN General Assembly, where we are circulating our petition.

Please sign this petition, circulate it, and help us educate others on the principles of physical economy, which is not the same thing as the stock market and monetarism, but pertains to the productivity of the labor force, of the industrial capacities, of the whole of the creativity of the individual. We have to strengthen an understanding of what makes an economy strong, and that is a permanent increase in scientific and technological innovation, which must not be limited to one country, but it is the right of every country to have such access to science and technology.

It's a very fascinating moment, so join the Schiller Institute and get on board.

Schlanger: And organize your friends to join us every Thursday, so they, too, can hear an update from Helga, which will go a long way toward cutting through the flack that's thrown up by the so-called mainstream media, so that people can actually become effectively involved, not just in this moment of the midterm elections, but in the shaping of the next two or three generations.

Helga, is there anything else you want to cover?

Zepp-LaRouche: No. I think we should really get active!

Schlanger: OK. So we'll see you next week, Helga. And you, our audience, just got your marching orders: Get active!

'Die Gedanken sind frei . . .' Thoughts Are Free But We Have To Think for Ourselves!

by Helga Zepp-LaRouche, Chair of the German Political Party *Büso*, the Civil Rights Movement Solidarity

Sept. 29—Admittedly, it is not a simple matter for people in Germany—and not only there—to face the future with optimism, given the volume of bad news circulated daily by the mainstream media, and the recent weeks' unworthy spectacle offered by the politicians of the so-called *GroKo* (Grand Coalition)—which has now become more of a "little coalition." However, it is quite possible to grasp the complex strategic reality—provided that you yourself try to develop an independent understanding of the most important issues of our time. And that requires mental work.

Or is everything already totally clear in your mind: Trump, Putin, Xi Jinping and Kim Jong-un are all dictators—no need to know more about their intentions, that's already settled. And the women in America who suddenly created the #McToo movement are all heroic, suddenly-liberated Barbie dolls who are finally rising up against decades of sexual oppression; and, of course, Africans are poor because they do not want to develop. One could add many more prejudices to this list of unquestioned axioms.

A German reader, even if he reads ten daily newspapers from *Bild* to *FAZ* and watches the news programs *Tagesschau* and *Heute*, would have no chance of understanding the extremely exciting events at this year's UN General Assembly. The only thing that was reported about President Trump's UN speech was the laughter with which part of the assembly responded to his comment on the success of his term up to now. In reality, the most interesting thing about Trump's speech was the combination of his conscious rejection of "old dogmas, discredited ideologies, and so-called experts who have been proven wrong over the years, time and time again," with his vision of a better humanity, bound together by

its shared history and its work for a common future.

With this speech, Trump made clear to public opinion why the trans-Atlantic establishment has reacted so hysterically to his arrival in the White House: here is an American president who rejects the "rules of the club" of the ruling class, who thinks "outside of the box." And indeed, putting aside minor differences, Trump's vision of the patriots' love for their respective nations and the common future of humanity, is not so far removed from President Xi Jinping's "Chinese Dream" and his " Community of Common Destiny for the One Humanity."

However, when one considers Trump's UN speech in connection with the many complex diplomatic activities connected with his bilateral meetings on the sidelines, they belie the vicious image of him that his political opponents propagate.

Trump met, among others, with Korean President Moon Jae-in, who credited him with the lion's share of the success in the progress of relations with North Korea and the process of denuclearization. Moon underscored the intense cooperation he had maintained with Trump during these negotiations, during which Trump had become "more than a friend" to him, and in whom he had developed "total trust." Moon further expressed the hope that the process of reconciliation with North Korea could be crowned this year with a peace treaty and the reunification of the two Koreas.

For his part, Russian Foreign Minister Lavrov added that Russia would do everything in its power to guarantee the economic success of North Korea in a reunified Korea. Japanese Prime Minister Abe stressed in his UN speech that he hopes to conclude a peace agreement between Japan and Russia before the end of this year, which would greatly improve the conditions for peace and stability throughout East Asia.

Reunification of Korea and a peace agreement between Japan and Russia by the end of the year? Trump "more than a friend" for President Moon? Did you know that, and does that fit into your image of Trump and your understanding of how the New Silk Road spirit has already changed relations between nations in Asia? If not, then complain to *Tagesschau* and Co.

However, Trump's incrimination of Iran as the main sponsor of terrorism in the world, is an outrageous statement, given the war of annihilation waged against Yemen by Saudi Arabia, and the decades of involvement by the U.S. with terrorist organizations ever since Zbigniew Brzezinski launched the "Islamic card" in Afghanistan in the 1980s against the Soviet Union. But on the other hand, Trump in effect supported the compromise negotiated by Putin and Erdogan in Sochi to create a buffer zone in Idlib, Syria, and thus to put a damper on the impending escalation between the armed forces of five nations, namely Turkey, Syria, Russia, the USA, and Israel—the latter three of which are nuclear powers. Trump expressly thanked the heads of state who had promoted the Astana process for Syria—including Iran.

For months, there has been talk of an overall peace plan for Southwest Asia, whose elaboration Trump has initiated. This is a mammoth task, given the complexity of the region and its character as a battlefield for imperial scenarios of the "Great Game" of the British Empire. But here, too, a facet of Trump's diplomacy is visible, although completely ignored in the black-and-white painting of the mainstream media: the Italian newspaper *La Verità* reported in this context on the possibility that Italy could play a mediating role in the current negotiations between the U.S. and Iran. Italian Prime Minister Giuseppe Conte, who met with Trump on the sidelines of the UN General Assembly for a bilateral meeting, represents the only major Western country that has built a very good relationship with Trump and at the same time established excellent ties to China, which, of course, significantly influences the dynamics around Iran.

As you can see here too, gray and pastel shades are more appropriate when considering Trump's policy than the shrill neon colors used by the media.

Both the spokesperson for the Russian Foreign Ministry, Maria Zakharova, and China, welcomed Trump's emphasis on the sovereignty of all nations, emphatically stressing that this right must apply not only to the U.S., but to all. In fact, this claim to sovereignty is diametrically opposed to the policy of interventionist encroachment, with which the U.S. administration often believes that U.S. law can be enforced extraterritorially anywhere in the world. That holds for example for the secondary sanctions that the United States imposes on foreign companies that are unwilling to submit to U.S. sanctions against Russia, China and Iran. The Chinese pro-government *Global Times* newspaper emphasized that both the principle of sovereignty and the equality of nations emerged from the process of the Peace of Westphalia, and that it is urgent to return to this principle in international relations.

The most problematic aspect of Trump's speech is the fact that he based his claims for the success for his economic policies mainly on the rise of stock market indices—a "success" that could be swept away at any moment with the outbreak of a new financial crisis, worse than that of 2008. And the U.S. trade deficit with China is not primarily attributable to China's accession to the WTO, but goes back to the policy of the New York Council of Foreign Relations and the Trilateral Commission in the 1970s, when they initiated the so-called "1980s Project" to elaborate and explicitly implement the "controlled disintegration of the global economy." Linked to this was the utopia of a "post-industrial society," and the outsourcing of production to low-wage countries, as China was then. Whole regions in the U.S., in and beyond the so-called "rust belt" of the Midwest, bear witness to the consequences of this fundamentally oligarchic, neoliberal policy.

Incidentally, the state of North Rhine-Westphalia, the former industrial center of Germany, is another sad expression of this policy of willful deindustrialization.

It is extremely important for us in Germany, given the devastation of the "Little Coalition," and the complete lack of any clear perspective for the future coming from Merkel's chancellorship, to attain a differentiated and independent picture of Trump, Russia, China and other important issues. It should be obvious to every thinking person that world peace depends on, above all, the USA, Russia, China, and then other important nations, such as India, Japan, etc., being able to establish a positive basis for cooperation. And that's why we should replace the clichés produced by the mainstream media on behalf of the geopolitical establishment's interests, with our own independent judgment. As I said: "Thoughts are free …"—but only if we ourselves think.

—zepp-larouche@eir.de

Why and How Europe Killed Its Own High-Speed Transportation Plans

by Karel Vereycken

Sept. 29—When considering the breathtaking expansion of high-speed rail networks in China—including its ambitious plans for the construction of maglev systems—it may come as a shock to learn that more than forty years ago, it was Europe that was leading the way in the development of these advanced technologies. France, Germany, Italy and Britain were all pushing the envelope for the creation of a Europe-wide, 21st Century

Transrapid 08 maglev train, at the Emsland Test Facility, in Emsland, Germany.

transportation system, and were poised for the development and deployment of maglev and related systems. Yet almost all of these efforts were systematically shut down. Why?

A fresh look at the archives—the 1978 Working Papers of the Strasbourg-based Parliamentary Assembly of the Council of Europe[1]—provides insights into why European states scrapped the very best of their national research on the new revolutionary technologies that were being spun off from the aerospace programs of the Kennedy era.

As I will demonstrate, the archives indicate that this was done, top-down, in great secret, in the name of European "unity," demanding that each nation sacrifice its own scientific contribution, however valuable it might be!

Typical was the sabotage of the Transrapid, the German-developed high-speed monorail train using magnetic levitation, for which planning started in 1969. This technology's most advanced version, the Transrapid 09, could reach a cruising speed of 500 km/h (311 mph), and had extremely rapid acceleration and deceleration.

Some time earlier, a brilliant French engineer, Jean Bertin—using an aerodynamic principle called "ground effect"—developed a Tracked Air Cushion Vehicle (TACV) in the late 1960s called "Aérotrain," a train without wheels, levitated by air-cushions and propelled

---

1. The Council of Europe (not to be confused with the European Council, on which sit the heads of state and heads of government), is a 47-nation international organization (much larger than the European Union) dedicated to upholding human rights, democracy and the rule of law. The Council of Europe is an older and wider circle of nations than the 28-member EU—it includes, for example, Russia and Turkey among its member states.

The debates on transportation took place in one of its bodies, the Parliamentary Assembly of the Council of Europe (PACE). Made up of 324 members drawn from the national parliaments of the Council of Europe's member states, PACE generally meets four times a year for week-long plenary sessions in Strasbourg. It is one of the two statutory bodies of the Council of Europe, along with the Committee of Ministers, the executive body representing governments, with which it holds an ongoing dialogue.

by an electric linear induction motor whose magnetic fields interact with a passive metallic rail. Prototypes of the Aérotrain broke world records, attaining 345 km/h as early as 1967 and 422 km/h in 1969!

During the same period, in the UK, a British rail engineer, Professor Eric Laithwaite, worked on the same principles and invented the Hovertrain, also a tracked hovercraft, while in Italy, the Aeronautical Institute of Palermo developed several prototypes of its own for air-cushion levitated vehicles, notably the IAP3.

CC/FlyAkwa

Aérotrain 180 prototype, on a test track near Saran, France, 1974.

Jean Bertin

A Polycentric European Capital?

The idea of a polycentric European capital, united by high-speed transport, is part of the relevant background. Since the very creation of the European Economic Community (EEC), the choice of the capital for Europe-wide institutions was and remains a subject of dispute. The European Commission and European Council are based in Brussels, Belgium, while the European Parliament is based in Strasbourg, France, but has a secretariat in both Luxemburg and Brussels. The European Atomic Energy Community (Euratom) is based in Brussels, while the European Organization for Nuclear Research (CERN) is in Geneva, Switzerland. It is an utterly mad arrangement.

In the early seventies, some people hoped to end this confusion with a polycentric capital of Europe under the name of Europolis. For such a capital to function, they proposed to interconnect, as soon as possible, the main cities housing European institutions with a single 800 km high-speed transportation corridor, also called Europolis or in French, Europole, stretching from Brussels to Geneva, via Liège, Luxembourg, Metz, Nancy, Strasbourg, Mulhouse, Basel, Lausanne and Bern. Travel speed was planned at 300 km/h, allowing a trip from Brussels to Geneva in three hours (today six hours).

Europole became very popular, not only among high-level EU technocrats, but also among local elected officials of Alsace and Lorraine, in a context in which the latter region, hit by the Davignon Plan reducing EU steel production (adopted in 1978), was desperately fighting to attract new economic activity.

A huge debate broke out, and in January 1971, the Council of Europe adopted resolution 471 (Document 2903, paragraph 6) calling for the creation of the Europole high-speed system.

In 1978, the Working Papers of the Council of Europe (Document 4096) summarized the debates in the section titled, "Europolis, a Factor for European Polycentrism" (page 34) as follows:

Few proposals of the Committee on Regional Planning and Local Authorities have aroused such controversy, in some cases very heated controversy, as the proposed high-speed air-cushion link connecting up the headquarters of European and international institutions (Brussels-Luxembourg-Strasbourg-Basle-Geneva), known as the "Europolis" project....

The Committee's proposals regarding this link-up between the headquarters of the European institutions were incorporated by the Assembly in its Resolution 471 (paragraph 6), which stated clearly that it would be a first link in a wide coordinated European network of high-speed land communications using a new technique (air-cushion) with a view of backing up railway networks whose main lines were already over-stretched and did not permit the high speeds now possible due to advanced techniques ... Mr.

Messmer, the [Gaullist] French Prime Minister at that time [1973], had stated several months before: "This project seems to me to be one of the most intelligent and of great value to our country and to Europe as a whole."

After quoting a study indicating that "present demand on the Europolis axis shows that total custom is small," the report goes on, saying the survey "endorses our program":

EIRNS/Stanley Ezrol

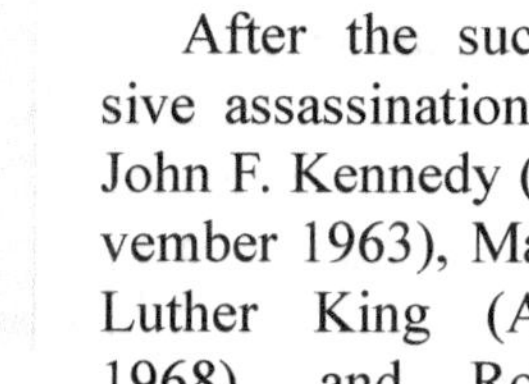

Club of Rome Chairman Alexander King.

Club of Rome President Aurelio Pecci.

UN

The single, central capital is a thing of the past. The concentration of European institutions in a single place would inevitably lead to centralization on a European scale. The disadvantages of dispersion can nowadays be resolved by modern means of transport and communication.

The report then goes through several cost-benefit analyses, demonstrating that the project was both sound and profitable, and concludes,

that at this stage no decision regarding the technology to be applied has as yet been made. For this preliminary study, the technological and economical data of the air-cushion system were adopted but a comparison with other technologies including the German technology of electrodynamic and electromagnetic suspension with linear motors will be made before any definite decision is taken.

Thus, Europe appeared to be poised to move into a maglev future.

Financial Deregulation and Malthusianism

In reality, the European enthusiasm for new modes of transport technologies provoked a terrific reaction among the financial oligarchy, an oligarchy that was then engaged in imposing a vicious, global financial dictatorship, whose power depended on the enforcement of Malthusian, anti-progress policies on a world scale.

After the successive assassinations of John F. Kennedy (November 1963), Martin Luther King (April 1968), and Robert Kennedy (June 1968), and the ousting of German Chancellor Konrad Adenauer (1963) and French President Charles de Gaulle (1969), the way was wide open for the British oligarchy and its friends and allies to impose a paradigm shift in world directionality, including the shutting down of the U.S. Apollo space program, the reversal of America's and Europe's commitment to advanced technology and scientific development, and the simultaneous imposition of a global regime of financial deregulation.

On the financial plane, the first large crack in the system appeared in 1967, with a run on gold and an attack on the British pound, provoking a 14.3% devaluation of the pound. Next, U.S. President Richard Nixon—breaking with the international financial system President Franklin Roosevelt had crafted at Bretton Woods, New Hampshire in 1944 took the United States off the gold reserve system in 1971. By late 1973, the regulated financial system had disintegrated, and participating currencies were allowed to float freely.

In the same time period, in 1968, former NATO operatives Aurelio Peccei and Alexander King founded the Malthusian Club of Rome, whose report, *The Limits to Growth*, called for zero growth to be imposed on both populations and economies, allegedly to prevent over-

Hovertrain RTV 31.

population and the depletion of existing resources. In order to impose this Malthusian post-industrial paradigm, scientific discoveries and new technologies such as nuclear energy were systematically demonized. The 1973 oil shock was mainly organized to brainwash populations into believing that growth should be halted or scaled down due to the rapid depletion of resources.

This rapid shift in both policies and outlook prepared the ground for the termination of Europe's nascent maglev systems.

Pragmatic Short-Sightedness

In France, the engineer Louis Armand, at that time (1955-58) the Chairman of the French national railway company (SNCF), was called in by French President de Gaulle's office. De Gaulle told him: "Do you realize that engineer Jean Bertin made a remarkable invention with his Aérotrain?" Rather than take this up as a challenge to revolutionize France's transit systems, Armand returned to his office and reportedly told his team: "Look guys, there's a guy who launched a crazy thing, a train on air cushions speeding over 300 km/h. If we don't come up with something, once this thing is flying, the SNCF is dead." His engineers responded: 'You know, we are preparing something simple, which consists of ramping up the speed of trains on rails, the *Train à Grande Vitesse* (TGV) [High-Speed Train]."

Denying the complementary role that normal rail and air-cushion/maglev transport could perform, the rail technocrats stuck to their old axioms. They rejected the development of maglev in favor of wheel-on-rail technology, as demonstrated in this contribu-

tion of the Paris-based International Union of Railways (IUR), of which Louis Armand was a president, to the debate appearing in the Working Papers:

> The prospects opened up by new technologies offering the possibilities of high cruising speeds with wheel-less guided transport systems (Aérotrain, Hovertrain, etc.) were regarded as a direct challenge by the railway authorities. They reacted in various ways, particularly by proposing substantially faster transport and comfort up to airline standards. But their ambitions did not end there. In the midst of the oil crisis, the European railway boards' IUR proposed in April 1973 a master plan for the future of European railways. This plan entails providing a homogeneous high-speed European rail network, capable of competing with air transport by 1985. The implementation of this plan should halve present traveling times between European cities. The new network would be to railways what motorways are to the rest of the road system. It is striking that this plan embraces the idea of a coherent European network, *though confined to one mode of transport.* [emphasis added]

The Master Plan proposed the upgrading of 13,593 km of existing railway and construction of some 5,875 km of new, high-speed rail—in total some 20,000 km of rail grid,[2] including a tunnel between France and Eng-

____
2. Still today, less than half built; see below.

TGV in Tours, France, 1994.

land, allowing traveling speeds between 200 and 300 km/h, meaning doubling the then existing speeds.

Parallel to these developments in France, on January 29, 1973, the British government, through the actions of UK Prime Minister Margaret Thatcher's sidekick Michael Heseltine, who was Minister for Aerospace at the time, pulled the plug on the British Hovertrain. Then, in June 1974, a freshly elected French president, Valéry Giscard d'Estaing, scrapped the contract, already signed and agreed to by the French state under President Georges Pompidou, for an Aérotrain air-cushion track connecting Paris's La Défense business district with Cergy Pontoise, a new city then under construction 50 kilometers from Paris, where the European Space Agency was about to locate its headquarters.

In Germany, the Emsland Transrapid Test Facility for Transrapid maglev trains was completed in 1984, and the Transrapid technology was validated in 1991 by the German railway authorities in cooperation with various universities. Despite these breakthroughs, however, the Transrapid is today banned in Germany. Only a short track of 30.5 km operates today—in China, between Shanghai and its airport.

Top-Down Malthusianism

To understand what happened, one has to read both the 1983 speech of French MP Alain Chenard (at that time mayor of Nantes) before the Council of Europe, as well as the subsequent reactions. Ambitiously, Chenard proposed, on the model of Airbus, to create a single European railway company of which the national railway companies (SNCF, Bundesbahn, etc.) would be shareholders. This new company would then be in charge of proposing a European transport technology integrating the advantages of both air cushion and maglev: "It would be unthinkable, said Chenard, that the new technology of tomorrow's Europe would be French, German, Belgian, or from Luxembourg. It will be European, or it will not be."

Subsequently, the Council of Europe buried Chenard's proposal, instead issuing an "Advice" (Opinion 23, paragraph i.), calling for—

Germany's Transrapid—banned in Germany.

a full feasibility study of the Europolis line, covering every aspect and comparing the merits of the various technologies, namely the TGV system [on wheels], magnetic levitation with linear induction motor (Transrapid), and air-cushion suspension (Aérotrain). A separate, detailed study should be made of each of these technologies; it should not be confined to the Strasbourg-Luxembourg-Brussels section, since that is only the first concrete manifestation of a purposeful, political scheme to build a central line of communication (London-Lille-Brussels-Liège-Luxembourg-Metz-Nancy-Strasbourg-Basel-Zurich-Milan) which would give Europe a polycentric structure, and might include extensions and ramifications in the directions of Rotterdam-Amsterdam, Paris, Cologne-Düsseldorf, Saarbrücken-Frankfurt, Karlsruhe-Stuttgart-Munich, Berne-Geneva-Lyons, etc.

And, paragraph "m" of the same Advice states that the feasibility study should "include the Europolis project in its program for the development of transport infrastructures of Community [EEC] interest," before concluding that, "in the short term, the improvement to this line proposed by the railway networks in question should also receive Community support."

All of this is double-speak for burying Chenard's maglev/Aérotrain proposal, and since European governments failed to act in a coherent fashion, the financial and Malthusian predators, mainly operating out of the City of London through EU institutions and bureaucracies, ended up imposing the worst. Not only did they destroy their own revolutionary innovations, but the promised upgrading of the railway grid never happened either. Instead of the promised 20,000 km, today only 9,000 km has been built or upgraded!

So, from the contextual evidence, one can conclude that, for the supreme sake of "European unity," Germany, France and others were arm-twisted by the "European deep state," actually the Anglo-Dutch financial oligarchy, to abandon their new revolutionary technologies such as maglev and air cushion, all of them based on the use of higher energy flux-densities, and to remain with "normal" rail transit systems, with the promise that speeds would be increased.

'No European High-Speed Rail Network Exists'

In June 2018, a special report of the European Court of Auditors observed, "Since 2000, the EU has provided 23.7 billion euros of co-funding to support high-speed rail infrastructure investments." However, they say,

> We found that the EU's current long-term plan is not supported by credible analysis, is unlikely to be achieved, and lacks a solid EU-wide strategic approach. Although the length of the national high-speed rail networks is growing, the Commission's 2011 target of tripling the number of kilometers of high-speed rail lines by 2030 will not be reached: 9,000 km of high-speed lines are currently in use, and around 1,700 km of line was under construction in 2017. On average, it takes around 16 years for new high-speed lines to proceed from the start of work to the beginning of operations.

Therefore, says the report:

> There is no European high-speed rail network, and the Commission has no legal tools and no powers in the decision making to ensure that

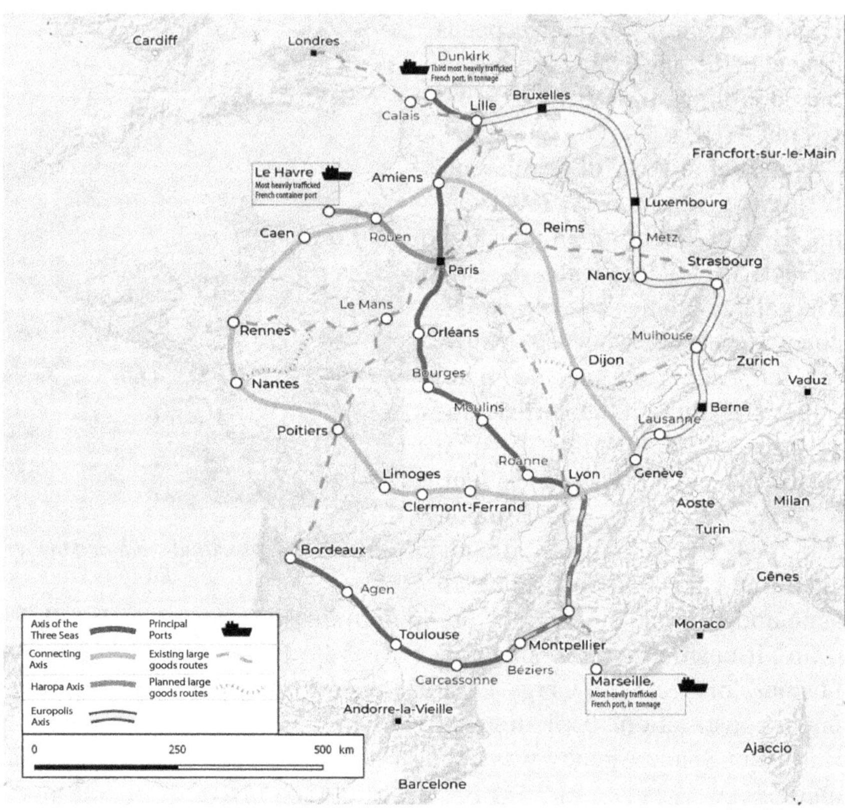

Karel Vereycken

Map showing the proposed, but never-built, 800 km Europolis system connecting London-Lille-Brussels-Liège-Luxembourg-Metz/Nancy-Strasbourg-Basel-Zurich-Milan, would give Europe a polycentric structure.

Member States make rapid progress toward completing the core network corridors set out in the TEN-T Regulation. As a result, there is only a patchwork of national high-speed lines, planned and built by the Member States in isolation. This patchwork system has been constructed without proper coordination across borders: high-speed lines crossing national borders are not amongst the national priorities for construction, even though international agreements have been signed and provisions have been included in the TEN-T Regulation requiring core network corridors to be built by 2030. This means a low EU added value of the EU co-funding of high-speed rail infrastructure investments.

There Is Hope—In a New Paradigm

Today, three new developments tend to make us optimistic and convince us that things might change very soon:

1. China, in merely a decade, has constructed some 20,000 km of high-speed rail, and now intends to shift

from its second generation TGV to its own maglev technology.

2. In France, a small but very serious start-up named Spacetrain is developing a new hydrogen powered, air-cushion high-speed vehicle.

3. Among the EU governments, the fear of the rise of popular outcry could cause them to finally deliver on the promises made 50 years ago. The immediate construction of the Europole fast-train connection could and should become their priority.

All of this can only become a reality in the framework of a New Bretton Woods system, a new Glass-Steagall law, and a return to Hamiltonian and Listian state credit, as elaborated and called for by the international LaRouche movement.

During the entirety of the period under discussion here, as European oligarchs acted to destroy maglev technology and deindustrialize Europe, the LaRouche movement actively and continually exposed the Malthusian nature of British designs, while also putting forward both scientific and economic policies which would return Europe (and the world) to a pathway of rapid physical-economic development. The only serious attempt in recent times to return Europe to infrastructure investment in the tradition of Friedrich List and Charles de Freycinet, began with the proposal for a "Productive Triangle," developed by Lyndon and Helga Zepp-LaRouche after the fall of the Berlin Wall in 1989, proposing to mobilize the core industrial capacity of Europe—whose center of gravity is located in the historically industrial area between Paris, Berlin and Vienna—to reconstruct and "irrigate" both Eastern Europe and Africa with mutually beneficial economic development.

The core of this proposal, now 30 years old, remains valid today. Furthermore, the recent advancement of China's Belt and Road Initiative is the outcome of what the LaRouches proposed now 30 years ago.

Nothing in a positive direction of significant magnitude is to be expected, however, while the trans-Atlantic banking and financial sector is being crushed under the burden of trillions of dollars of unpayable speculative debt, especially about 1 to 2 quadrillion dollars of worthless derivatives. This reality emphasizes the urgency for convening a New Bretton Woods monetary conference, for the purpose of averting worldwide financial disaster and returning to a system where the issuance of credit is tied to productive investment. Under such an arrangement, maglev, Aérotrain, Transrapid, and much more will become possible.

NEW RELEASE, **Volume II**

The New Silk Road Becomes the World Land-Bridge:

A Shared Future For Humanity

The spirit of the New Silk Road is changing the world for the better. The exciting overview in this new 440-page Volume II report updates the roadmap given in Volume I, on the coming into being of the World Land-Bridge for development and peace. BRICS countries have a strategy to prevent war and economic catastrophe. It's time for the rest of the world to join!

Includes:
Introduction by Helga Zepp-LaRouche, "A Shared Future for Humanity."

Progress Reports on development corridors worldwide, spurred by China's Belt and Road Initiative. Features 140 maps.

Principles of Physical Economy by Lyndon LaRouche, especially his "Four Laws" for emergency action in the Trans-Atlantic.

Soft cover (440 pages)
Domestic Price: $60. Shipping cost included in price.
Foreign Price: $60. Add $15 per copy for shipping.
Order from **newparadigm.schillerinstitute.com**
Tel 1 703 297 8368

NOVEMBER 30, 1994

On the Recovery from the Impending Financial Collapse

by Lyndon H. LaRouche, Jr.

The following was delivered as the keynote speech to a conference on international development, sponsored by the Schiller Institute in Washington, D.C. on Nov. 30, 1994.

You may have noticed that the United States recently had a mid-term election, which was, from the standpoint of anyone knowing what's going on behind the scenes, really inconclusive. What we've seen surfacing in the United States, behind people like Sen. Phil Gramm [R-Tex.] and others, is a revival of something which we last saw conspicuously in Europe, notably in Germany, during the 1920s and 1930s.

There is a rather famous book written by a veteran of that period, Dr. Armin Mohler, a Swiss former volunteer for the Waffen SS, resident in Munich, in which he brags about his trying to dissociate himself from Hitler, while bragging about what he was a part of, the thing that Mr. Newt Gingrich [R-Ga.] is proud to be a part of today. It was called the "Conservative Revolution." The Nazis in Germany were one part of the Conservative Revolution, of course; but the Nazis were only one of about 100 organizations in Europe, which all belonged, in that period, to the category of Conservative Revolution, which is a much more accurate term than the generic and loosely used term "fascist."

At the end of the war, one branch of the Conservative Revolution was organized under the sponsorship of Winston Churchill in Switzerland. That organization was called the Mont Pelerin Society, and its leader, until 1992 when he died, was a fascist by the name of Friedrich von Hayek, who was the man who confused the word "fascism" with freedom, and "free trade" with prosperity.

The notable feature of the Conservative Revolution, which has been around in the United States, as an endemic problem, for a long time, is fascism. Milton Friedman is an example of a fascist, in the strictest sense of the Conservative Revolution.

But the thing that brought the fascist vote out (not implying that all Republicans are fascists, by any means), was the fact that the United States, like most of the world, is going through an experience which is comparable to that which Germany went through during the 1920s. Unlike Germany of the 1920s, we have not really lost any wars recently. We may have fought a few we shouldn't have fought, but we have not lost any, conspicuously. We're not under the occupation of anybody but the British and the United Nations Organization.

But economically, culturally, and socially, a growing percentile of our people in the United States are demoralized and enraged, for reasons quite similar to the spread of demoralization and rage in Central Europe, and also in France, during the 1920s and 1930s.

So, we will have, under these circumstances, what I believe you will see, is the temporary eruption of a leading fascist organization, headed by Newt Gingrich, called the "Squeaker of the House." This typifies the fact that we're in a crisis.

What has happened, is that over the recent period, government has stopped working—government *no longer works.* Government generally, in Europe and North America and elsewhere, is a failure. The collapse of the Soviet and Warsaw Pact system in 1989 to 1991, was simply a reflection on the communist side, of what is a worldwide breakdown of the kinds of systems which were built up during the postwar period, but especially a breakdown of the new institutions which began to emerge between 1964 and 1968 in the United States, western Europe, and elsewhere.

The prevailing axioms of politics all consistently fail. The politicians say, "Well, we have to perfect our policy, to be consistent with our axioms. If free trade fails, we've got to have a stronger dose of free trade, even if it kills us."

The policies which people think are the cures or the remedies for our affliction, are in fact the policies which, under these circumstances, are ruining us. It's like the fellow who insisted on taking a certain road to work every day, even after the bridge had blown out.

What we've come to is an indication of what the nature of this crisis is, which grips the entire planet, but most notably those sections of the planet which are deemed the dominant or most powerful sections, including the United States.

One might say that the problem of the U.S. political process, is that the think-tanks and politicians, with a few exceptions, have not got a clue as to what's going on; and everything they do, because of their ignorance, and because of their misguided beliefs, will turn out to be a terrible mistake. And the voters, who were very angry, did not really vote *for* Mr. Gingrich and his type; they voted *against* anybody who was in office, out of rage, frustration, and hopelessness.

The End of a Cycle of Civilization

What is actually happening may seem a bit complicated at first, but I hope I can make it clear to you. We're in the middle of the end of an entire dynastic cycle in modern western European civilization, which, of course, has become, because of its power, a worldwide civilization. Every part of the world is assimilated, in some degree or another, into western European civilization, as it emerged over the period from about 1440 A.D. to about 1600 A.D. It is that civilization, that dominant civilization, which is in the process of collapsing.

The Sequoyah nuclear plant of the Tennessee Valley Authority, whose creation helped the United States get out of the Great Depression of the 1930s. By putting $1-2 trillion into circulation, on the basis of loans, through a national banking institution, to federal, state, and local public utilities—through work, not through throwing money out in the street—you generate the basis for a general revival of the U.S. economy.

In ancient and and medieval times, one spoke, especially in Asia, of dynastic cycles. We remember the dynasties of China, the dynasties of the subcontinent of Asia, the dynasties of Mesopotamia, the dynasties of Canaan, the dynasties of Egypt. The dynasty of Rome, which is the Asiatic model, again.

We study, of course, the rise and fall or the rise and decline, of these dynastic cycles. We are now coming to the close of a dynastic cycle which, in point of fact, is about 500 or more years old. The cycle began with a collapse of the previous form of society in Europe, a collapse which occurred *officially* about 1350 A.D., when the existing financial and banking system of Europe, which was involved in a large debt bubble somewhat similar to the worldwide derivatives speculative bubble today, blew out.

When the king of England discovered that he was guilty of seducing his creditors into the mortal sin of usury by continuing to pay usurious loans, he decided to try to help save his creditors' souls by repudiating the sinful debt. That resulted in a collapse of the two leading banking houses of Europe at the time, the Bardi and Peruzzi, and immediately, the entire banking system of Europe collapsed. As a matter of fact, it *disintegrated.*

We are now facing something similar. The disintegration of our civilization became obvious from about 1964-68. Those of you who have studied the experience of developing nations—and some have come from there, and so they know something about it—recognize that, in the middle of the 1950s, until the assassination of John F. Kennedy in the United States, at least the lip-service policy of the United Nations and of the leading nations of the world, was the policy which was that of President Franklin Roosevelt during the Second World War.

The policy of Roosevelt was, that what would be called today the developing nations, should be freed from slavery to British and other forms of imperialism and colonialism, and that these nations had the right to develop. They had the right to access to the technology by which they could meet their own needs, and take equal standing in the community of sovereign nation-states.

Churchill violently opposed the policy, and, much to Churchill's gratification, Roosevelt died in 1945, and a man who was more tractable to the ideas of London, Harry Truman, took office.

But, despite the fact that Truman betrayed, in effect, the policies of his predecessor, Mr. Roosevelt, and capitulated to Churchill, nonetheless, as a veteran of that period, coming back from India and Burma at the end of that war, I can attest to the fact that most of we returning veterans, particularly those who had seen something of Asia as well as Europe, recognized, in the condition and the oppression of the peoples of Asia, that if we did not cure this problem and bring economic and related justice to the peoples of these oppressed areas, that we were leaving one war to plant the seeds of another.

This was the general mood of we among the returning veterans who came to political power and leadership in the United States at about the time that Kennedy became President. And we were for economic justice toward the developing sector, just as we generally supported the ideas that Kennedy is associated with, whether or not we agreed with him on his marital behavior, or whatever else. The man represented a generation of which we were a part. The civil rights legislation in the United States was not merely a product of the civil rights movements, as led by great people, including a genius by the name of Martin Luther King; but the success of the civil rights movement was not due to the struggles of the African-American, because African-Americans had been struggling for freedom in the United States for more than two centuries before then.

The reason was, that the African-American, under good leadership, found, in the returning veteran from World War II, then coming to power in the United States, a responsive leadership which was sympathetic to that cause. And so, during that period of the 1950s and the early 1960s, it was considered *only just* that the people of the developing countries should have a right to access to technology and the other trappings of national sovereignty, to attain their dignity, and to build a community on this planet of sovereign nation-states, which would be the precondition for peace.

This was reflected in the United Nations Organization's First Development Decade. The last gasp of that Development Decade policy appeared in the middle of the 1960s, when U Thant, then the U.N. secretary general, issued a Second Development Decade proposal, which was the last time that anybody in the U.N., in the officialdom, or anybody in the metropolitan countries, in terms of governments, seriously proposed that the industrialized countries of the planet, should make it a mission to bring the underdeveloped countries of this planet, into full access to the technologies, to the science, to the development, which would make them independent nations standing on parity with the other nations on this planet.

Renaissance Institutions

During the period 1964-68, the period of the Vietnam War's anti-war movement, and such things, a change occurred. This civilization, whose power rested upon institutions established during the Renaissance in about 1440, had built three kinds of new institutions which transformed this planet. One was the idea of the *sovereign nation-state under law.* Not a nation ruled as a tribe, not a nation ruled by a ruling family, not groups of people who are under the domination of some ruling group, but that the people, the families, the population of a nation, should constitute themselves collectively as a nation-state under law according to principles of law, and according to a common form of literate language. Because if you don't have a literate language, you cannot communicate important ideas; and if you cannot communicate important ideas in a common language, you cannot deliberate important matters. And if you cannot deliberate important matters, you *cannot rule yourself,* you cannot participate efficiently in government. You can vote for this or that, but you cannot deliberate the policies efficiently upon which the life or death of your nation may depend.

The second thing, in addition to the nation-state form, was the establishment of modern science. Now, modern science actually began, even though it has roots way back, including Plato and the Academy of Athens over the 200 years approximately from 400 B.C. to 200 B.C., in the fifteenth century. Modern science in a general way was established by a book written by one of the founders of the Council of Florence, Nicolaus of Cusa, called *De Docta Ignorantia,* or *On Learned Ignorance.* This book established the principles of method of modern science.

Cusa and the others who established modern science, also established the commitment of the nation-state to the betterment of the condition of mankind, through the fostering and realization of scientific and technological progress, in order to uplift the condition of mankind as an individual, and in families. And it was on that basis, that this curve (see **Figure 1,** top), that you see in the chart, was realized.

Prior to 1440 A.D., on this planet, through the 2 million years or so previously that mankind is known to have existed on this planet, the human race never exceeded a population of about several hundred million persons at the maximum. That is, the potential population density of this planet, was limited both by natural conditions, and by the inability of the human species to make enough progress, to break that barrier of several hundred million.

Much worse, the condition of mankind until the European Renaissance, throughout this planet, was mostly bestial. Ninety-five percent or more of the population of all parts of this planet lived in serfdom, slavery, or brutish toil of a similar form. Man was illiterate, barely surviving, subject to all kinds of cruelties and penalties and abuses. The entire development of mankind out of that condition of virtual bestialization for most of the population was the result of the benefits in the institution of the nation-state, the institution of science and cultural development of a similar type, and the institution of technological and scientific progress generally applied both to increase the productive powers of labor, to change the conditions of community and family life for the better, and a commitment by society to attempt to address its material problems of life, by means of finding the technologies to assist man in gaining the power to overcome disease, to overcome hunger, to increase the potential population density of this planet (see **Figure 1,** middle).

In point of fact, if we fully deployed the level of scientific knowledge which we had achieved at about 1968-69, we could sustain quite comfortably upon this planet 25 billion people with the standard of life approaching or reaching that which was enjoyed by the standard of a so-called typical American back in those years. We have the means.

The Oligarchy Versus Progress

That's not the limit. There is no limit to what we can do in scientific progress if we put our mind to it. But in 1964-68 there occurred what was called a "cultural paradigm shift." This cultural paradigm shift radiated from the British monarchy to an institution which is called today the World Wildlife Fund or the World Wide Fund for Nature, headed by Prince Philip. This organization is backed by and is an instrument of the most powerful oligarchical assembly in the world today, which is called commonly the Club of the Isles. In the Club of the Isles, the wealthiest and most powerful families in the world are assembled around the British monarchy.

The monarchy itself is very rich, vastly rich, through stealing things. That happened in the nineteenth and twentieth centuries. But the power behind the monarchy, which can kill the monarchs and replace them, is an oligarchy of forces, including the opium traders of the nineteenth century into China, that sort of crowd.

They decided that the time had come to bring to an end scientific and technological progress as a general practice, to bring to an end the desire of the former colonial countries, the so-called developing countries, for parity in development. They used sub-Saharan Africa as a test tube for genocide, and that is no exaggeration.

They introduced, among the youth of the 1960s and 1970s, a dumbing-down process. The students who graduated from universities after 1968, were less intelligent than those before. Not for biological reasons, but for educational reasons, and for cultural reasons. The students who graduated from high schools, universities, in the 1980s in Europe and the United States, are *vastly inferior* in every quality (with a few exceptions, of course, always), generally, to the graduates of high schools, secondary schools, and universities in the 1960s.

As a result of these policies, which were called ecology or post-industrial society policies, not only was the development of the so-called Third World halted; the developing sector was *looted,* denied the right to access to technology and looted at cheap prices. That was the late 1960s.

If you measure productivity and consumption in

Growth of European Population, Population-Density, and Life-Expectancy at Birth, Estimated for 100,000 B.C.–A.D. 1975

Alone among all other species, man's numerical increase is a function of increasing mastery over nature —increase of potential population-density—as reflected historically in the increase of actual population-density. In transforming his conditions of existence, man transforms himself. The transformation of the species itself is reflected in the increase of estimated life-expectancy over mankind's historical span. Such changes are primarily located in, and have accelerated over, the last six-hundred years of man's multi-thousand-year existence. Institutionalization of the conception of man as the living image of God the Creator during the Golden Renaissance, through the Renaissance creation of the sovereign nation-state, is the conceptual origin of the latter expansion of the potential which uniquely makes man what he is.

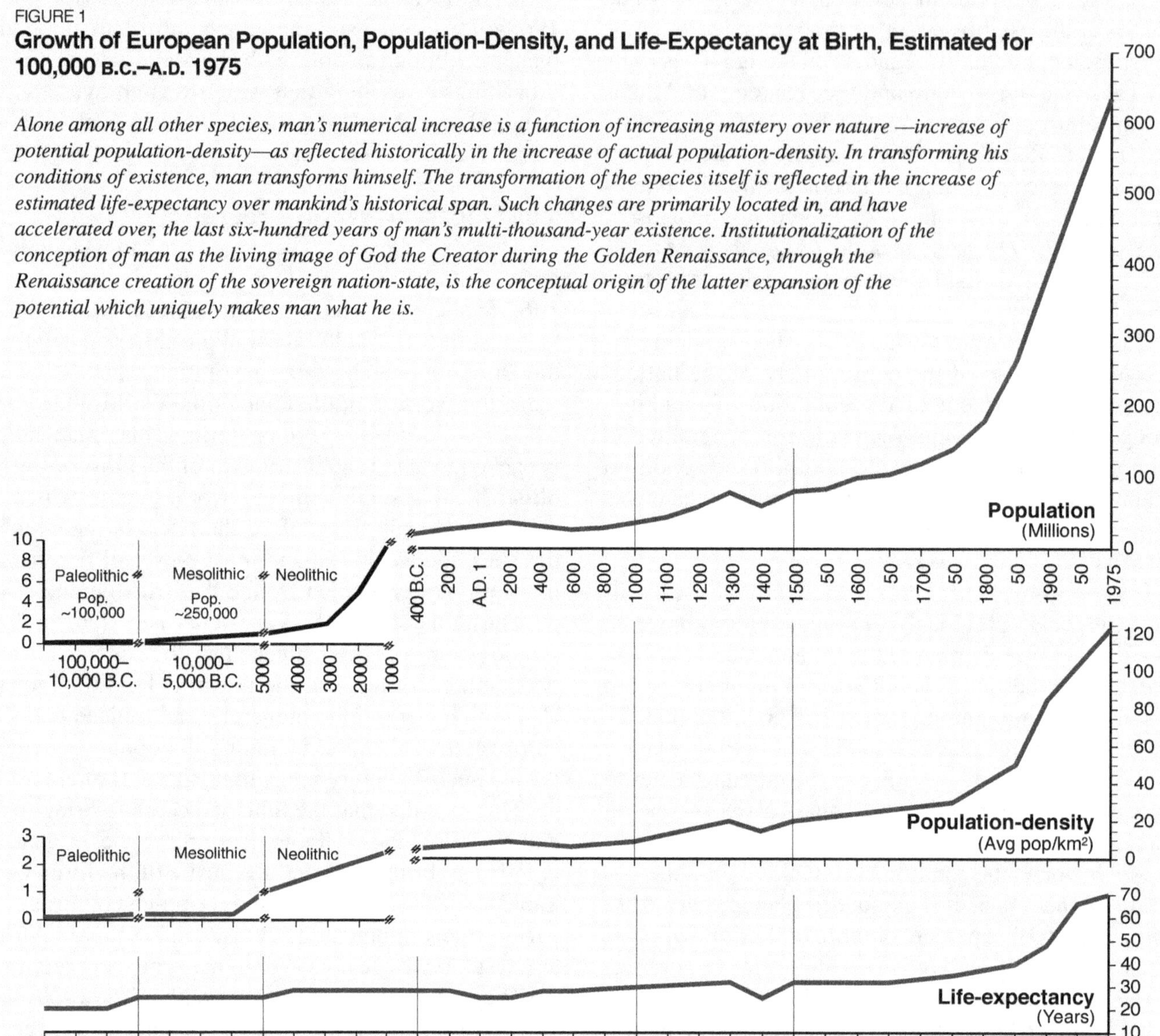

All charts are based on standard estimates compiled by existing schools of demography. None claim any more precision than the indicative; however, the scaling flattens out what might otherwise be locally, or even temporally, significant variation, reducing all thereby to the set of changes which is significant, independant of the quality of estimates and scaling of the graphs. Sources: For population and population-density, Colin McEvedy and Richard Jones, *Atlas of World Population History*; for life-expectancy, various studies in historical demography.

Note breaks and changes in scales.

terms of material consumption, plus education, plus health care, plus science and related services; if you measure that in terms of per capita for labor force, per household, and per square kilometer, the planet as a whole has been devolving economically over the past 25 years.

That is, the productive powers of labor, as measured in actual products and services, as opposed to prices, have been declining. The United States is decaying. The United States, by the early 1980s, could no longer have launched the Apollo Moon landing; we couldn't have done it. We had shut down whole categories of industry, and put out of business whole categories of technology which were essential to the successful Moon landing by the 1980s.

Today, we're in far worse shape.

All throughout the world, essential industries are collapsed and destroyed, and the per capita consumption in real terms, is far less per capita, per household, and per square kilometer. Our infrastructure, our rail systems, our water systems, our sanitation systems, have been decaying without repair. Our municipalities are becoming hellholes. This is obvious to us in the United States; it's also true in other parts of the world.

We have reached the limit of the ability to control resistant strains of infectious disease by means of antibiotics, and means of immunization; and yet, we have *halted* medical research. What is being done to the physician in the United States, is criminal. The physician in the United States, as a result of changes introduced in the past 15 to 17 years, is no longer legally permitted to follow his conscience in the treatment of his patients. This has been taken over by the malpractice rules, by the insurance companies, and so forth and so on.

The quality of health care available to the population today, is, by and large, *vastly inferior* to that available earlier, largely because government and other busybody agencies, and malpractice practices, have stripped away from the physician, the physician's right to practice medicine.

Since the percentage of the population which is actually producing wealth, has shrunken to below 20% of the labor force, as compared to 60% of the labor force at the end of World War II, fewer people are actually producing wealth. More people are simply parasites engaged in occupations which make no contribution to the well-being of society, such as the New York derivatives speculators: Who needs them? Such as these people playing with computers and chaos theory, to speculate and *loot* pension funds, to loot school budgets with their privatization programs, to take over corporations with hostile acquisitions, and to destroy the valuable corporations which are our industries, in order to loot profits to retire the debt which is incurred by the hostile takeover.

The condition of most of the developing world, is unspeakable. We have epidemics which are building up. We face a global biological holocaust potentially analogous to that which brought the population of Europe, in the middle of the fourteenth century, down to *half* of what the population of Europe had been, in the middle of the thirteenth century.

Famine and disease are destroying the populations of the world. What is happening in Africa, through famine, disease, and the activities of the World Wide Fund for Nature, and associated agencies, is a crime far worse than was made notorious in eastern Europe under Hitler. It is ongoing. We have faced a situation in Africa,

in which entire nations are about to be eliminated from the political map, by the biological consequences of the policies which have been practiced, in particular, over the past 25 to 35 years. That's the condition of humanity.

The Debt Swindle

In the early 1970s, another step was taken. The U.S. dollar collapsed in the spring and summer of 1971, when some swindlers advised President Richard Nixon to do a very stupid thing—but it wasn't stupid from their standpoint—to destroy the last remnant of stability of parities of currencies on a gold-reserve basis, and to go to what is called a floating exchange-rate monetary system.

The result of the floating exchange-rate monetary system was manifold, and this became worse and worse, especially over the 1972 period from the Azores Conference, through measures taken in the U.S. Congress in 1982, under George Bush's leadership in the Senate. What has happened, is the creation of an unearned debt against the developing nations and other nations, and to the advantage of speculators in the London market. How does it work?

Under a floating exchange-rate system, the currency of a country such as Brazil, is arbitrarily, through market manipulation, reduced way below its true value in purchasing power. Then the International Monetary Fund and other agencies come in, and tell the Brazilians, "You must reduce the value of your currency. Otherwise, you will not be deemed *creditworthy* in international markets." The Brazilians say, "Okay, fine, that means you will give us higher prices for our goods, than in our current currency, because they're worth more on the world market."

"No! You will price your goods in your domestic market at the *same* price as before. You will simply have to give us more of those goods now, to pay the debt, to meet the debt services."

"Well, we can't afford that."

This process began with what London orchestrated with the help of Henry Kissinger, which is called the "oil price hoax," in the middle of the 1970s, in which the price of petroleum was rigged. Developing nations could not afford to continue to pay these jacked-up prices, so they would borrow. The exchange-value of their currency would be dropped, and purely bookkeeping loans would be made, through which the nations received no credit, in fact, whatsoever, but were purely charged.

This is how the entirety of South and Central America has more than re-paid the entire debt it had in the early 1970s. And yet, the remaining debt is higher by far than it was then. This is also true in Africa. It's true in Asia; and it's also true in developed countries, such as the United States.

Debt service, created through a floating-exchange rate system, is eating away at real production. In point of fact, if you look at the U.S. economy and the European economies from a *physical* standpoint—that is, in terms of market baskets of physical consumption, market baskets as the measure of productivity per capita—actually, the economies of the United States, North America, and western Europe are operating at a deficit, at a loss. That is, they are using up more goods to operate than they are producing. These countries are living only by looting one another, by looting old assets, or by looting what we sometimes call the Third World.

From 1982 on, this floating-exchange rate system began to generate a massive bubble, a speculative financial bubble of the same general characteristic as that bubble which caused the collapse of the European banking system in the middle of the seventeenth century in Holland, or like the Mississippi Bubble, or like the South Sea Island Bubble in England and France, the so-called John Law Bubbles of the early eighteenth century. We now have a situation typified by the following: On the London financial market, or any other financial market generally in the world, there is a $1 trillion a day turnover, approximately, in financial transactions, of which less than 2% is accounted for in terms of commerce and trade.

Ninety-eight percent, 97% of transactions are purely speculation feeding the bubble. The policies of government, including the United States government, is to pay the debt to a Federal Reserve System which is creating fictitious cash to feed these bubbles. So what is happening, is that the real economy, that produces the machine tools, the food, the clothing, the housing, and so forth, that economy is being shrunk by austerity measures which are aiming to provide more wealth, to sustain the bubble. That is, a financial leverage against this stream of wealth, is what is used to keep the bubble alive.

The bubble is getting bigger, the economies are getting smaller; because every economy is *physically* operating at a loss, everything taken out of the economy to pay the bubble, is shrinking the economy.

It's like a situation of a man who has cancer, and the cancer is growing by eating him; it gets to the point that the cancer is bigger than he is, and unless the cancer can continue to be fed at the same rate, the cancer is going to die. *That* is the situation of the world economy, under the present circumstances.

As a guarantee of that, what we face now, is an imminent collapse of the global monetary and financial system. That collapse will come soon. It's highly probable, that this system will end within two years, by about the time of the next general election in the United States. It could collapse almost any morning. It could possibly be stretched slightly longer; that's a political question. But probably this thing is going to blow *before* the next general federal election in the United States, in 1996.

The system will collapse in any case. *Nothing can save the present global financial and monetary system.* It cannot be saved. It has no assets, it is already bankrupt. We can do nothing to save it. No matter how hard you tried, you couldn't save it. If you try to save it, you're just like the man who's already bankrupt, who starts embezzling to try to keep his firm alive when he can no longer salvage it. He's already bankrupt, he's just going to make it worse if he doesn't admit it, and that's the situation we're in.

Bankruptcy or Chaos

Now, the intelligent, rational thing to do, would be to have sovereign governments do their job, and to put the world's central banks, the banking systems, and the financial markets into bankruptcy reorganization under government supervision. That would prevent chaos, just the same way as any good bankruptcy proceeding with a bankrupt company, whether the company is saved or not, is a way of preventing or minimizing the social chaos and disruption which attends a bankruptcy.

The worst thing that can happen in a bankruptcy, is to let it run on, which causes chaos. Bankruptcy is a means of stabilizing a bad situation.

Government can prevent chaos, and keep institutions from being swept away, when government gets the guts to put the existing central banks, including the Federal Reserve System, which is bankrupt, and the International Monetary Fund and so forth, into formal bankruptcy reorganization under government supervision. That is necessary.

If that is not done, then you will have another kind of collapse. You will have a collapse which takes the form of what might be called a chain-reaction implosion, caused by what's called reverse leverage, which takes the following form: On one bright, sunny morning, people go to the markets, and the man on the street assumes that everything will be business as usual that week. Two to three days later, the financial institutions of the world will have virtually all disintegrated, because a collapse has occurred which has no bottom.

So we'll have either bankruptcy, and an orderly bankruptcy, or we will have chaos. And if chaos occurs without remedy, we could plunge the world into a New Dark Age.

Generally, in the history of dynasties, each time a dynasty of a culture has collapsed, there has been a protracted period of decades or even a century longer, in which the people of that culture go into what's called a New Dark Age, as western Europe at the collapse of the Roman Empire, or what happened in the fourteenth century, when the

TVA

A parade in 1934 celebrates the fact that Tupelo, Mississippi was the first city to sign a contract with the Tennessee Valley Authority for electric power development, in a program to get the nation out of the depression.

banking system collapsed, and about half the people of Europe died during the 100 years bridging that period, and about 30% of the population of Europe died in that period partly because of the bubonic plague. But the bubonic plague spread under conditions which were caused by the economic collapse.

We can go into a New Dark Age which can last on this planet well into the next century, if we allow chaos to take over. So, the question which confronts us today is: How do we address this crisis? How do we bring ourselves to recognize the failure of this system, that we're at the end of a dynasty, that all the old tricks don't work any more, that the ride is finished, the ship is sinking? If you try to cling to the ship and save it, you'll only drown yourself. You've got to get a new ship; and that's going to be the politics of the coming period.

Building a General Recovery Program

In my view, we now have to build a general economic recovery program for this planet, and that's what I wish to devote myself to. But let me just make a few more remarks on a couple of points before getting to the recovery program.

Let's look at the principle, first of all, which underlay the success of the Golden Renaissance. I'd mentioned earlier that, in ancient times, 90 to 95% of the population was treated within every culture, as virtually animals, peasant animals, mostly living in rural life.

What are peasants, in the mind of the oligarch? The peasant is the person who is like a little animal. He goes out and he manures a rock, and he grows crops. Ninety-five percent of the population are peasants, or similar people. They grow the food. They live in miserable conditions. But they provide the food upon which the small percentile of the population, with its labor, is able to maintain a culture.

So you have at the top, a very small group, an oligarchy. You have under them, people who help them administer society: military, bureaucrats, what not—lackeys. And under it, you have 95% of the population which is oppressed and bestialized.

Let me just identify why the Renaissance in Europe in the fifteenth century is so important to us today. What happened then? What happened in 1440 A.D., which caused a rate of growth of the population, which had stagnated at several hundred million people, suddenly to take off with hyperbolic growth? What made the growth extend through the development of Europe, despite all the troubles and tribulations which occurred there, such that the benefits of this culture were admired and sought out and adopted, sometimes not successfully, but desired, by most of the part of this planet?

Up until the middle or late part of the 1960s, every developing nation of this planet, no matter what its cultural origins, desired the right to access to the benefits of technological progress, and was being told, for part of the time, "Yes, you have a right, but it's going to be a little slow on delivery," or were then later told, "No."

Then Prince Philip said, "No. You black Africans are annoying my animals that I intend to hunt. So you're going to keep your population down," a Prince Philip who said he wished he could be reincarnated as a deadly virus so he could wipe out the excess people. And that's the policy of the World Wide Fund for Nature and the Club of the Isles.

Man in the 'Image of God'

So, what happened in the fifteenth century that's so important? Well, the principle here was very simple; very complicated, but very simple in conception. You find it, if you read about the beginning of this era, if you read the writings of a famous Hebrew scholar and also a banker by the name of Philo of Alexandria, Philo Judaeus, who wrote a series of papers which includes one on the account of creation given by Moses.

Philo says correctly and very clearly, that man is created in the image of God, as the First Book of Moses on creation says, by virtue of the fact that man, unlike any beast, has an intellectual power which mirrors the intellectual power of God. That is, not merely an intellectual power to contemplate, but an intellectual power to create new things, and to create true new things, not merely as ideas, as conversations, as opinions; but to take these ideas, bring them to nature, subdue nature, and produce a beneficial improved state of nature which never existed before. This is how man grew.

If man were an animal, without this intellectual power, the human population of this planet would never have exceeded several million people. Man has biologically, without this power, no more potential for growth of population than a baboon or a chimpanzee, approximately; and therefore, our condition of life, and our population numbers would never have exceeded that of approximately one of the higher apes but for this power.

So we know that every human being in every part of this planet, we can prove historically, has this remarkable creative power which no animal has; that the intellect of man attempts to *imitate* the intellect of God through creativity, to call things into existence physically, states of matter which never existed before, through this creative power. And this is what makes man special and sacred.

Philo and the early Christians taught that. St. Paul and St. Peter undertook an evangelizing mission among the slaves of the Roman Empire, and preached that all men, by virtue of being in the image of God, were equal before God, that you could no longer have categorically a division of society among rulers, lackeys, and slaves, because all men are equal.

Therefore, the just condition of the behavior of man toward man, is to look into the eyes of another person, and recognize that behind those eyes, lies the remarkable intellectual quality which makes that person in the image of God. Well, this was the Christian idea, it was the Augustinian Christian idea which took strong root in western Europe. *But until 1440,* this idea had never been put into practice as a principle of statecraft, of government.

The introduction of the idea of science and a nation-state committed to scientific progress for the benefit of every person and every family, was a new idea—the nation-state with responsibility for all.

For example, look in the U.S. Constitution's Preamble. The most important part of the U.S. Federal Constitution is in the Preamble: "to secure these blessing for ourselves and our posterity," the general welfare clause. What is the function of the individual? Our lives are short. They may be sometimes long for a child but as you get older, as we do, some of us, life gets shorter and shorter. The months spin past. And what's life about? It's for the contribution you make through family and society, to posterity. This is sometimes, as I said, called the general welfare. This does not mean put everybody on welfare; this means that the well-being of society is our concern. The New Age would have everybody on welfare, and then kill them by starving them to death.

So this idea was put into effect with the idea of the nation-state, as Cusa says, for example, that every nation has the right to share in the scientific discoveries of any other nation, free of charge. That's the principle of humanity. And that is what gave western European civilization its great power.

Ah, but it wasn't that simple. The people who represented that which the Renaissance attempted to overturn, the Venetian oligarchy, similar people who had run the old feudal imperialist type of society, objected to giving up their power.

As we know, on every part of this planet, you'll find people who believe that we must perpetuate a system in which 90% or 80% or 60% of the people must be underdogs, an underclass, people who believe that their right to enjoy luxury and idleness at the expense of poor people laboring in bestial or brutish toil, is the natural way of things.

This is the struggle within China. This is the struggle within India. This is the struggle throughout the world: to realize a form of society in which every individual is appreciated as being equal in importance, from the time of birth.

And these forces that didn't want that, fought, and they fought hard. And, as a result of a long history, which is a story in itself, those forces which opposed the Renaissance, which wanted to eliminate the nation-state as an institution, which wanted to create an imperial world government; these people have gained the greatest power, the financial power, and that's what our problem is today.

So, by our not freeing ourselves, as the American Revolution, for example, attempted to do and did with partial success (for which it was much admired in former times, before it began to get British ways and became less admired), we failed to free mankind of the overlordship of an oligarchy which is typified by the World Wide Fund for Nature and the Club of the Isles behind it today.

That's what our crime is. We have not succeeding in winning the conflict between the oligarchy and that which was good, the impulse to develop mankind, an impulse which was reflected in my generation and our support for the idea of the Development Decades.

But on the other side, the other forces have proven politically more powerful, partly because the ordinary people do not know what is in their own interest. And the ordinary people, as in the recent election in the United States, in many cases, went out and voted for an outright fascist. The senior citizen who voted for Newt Gingrich, unless he's very rich, is committing suicide.

Our problem is that we do not have institutions which have effectively mobilized the average person to understand his own true interest. This problem becomes more difficult when we don't have real education in our schools, because we have people on the streets who we can meet, we can look them in the eyes, and, within, they are good people; but they are so *poorly* educated, so *poorly* informed. They don't know anything. Their minds have not been developed. And they lack the ability to understand their problem.

So, those of us who do know, have the responsibility to act for the benefit of those who do not, and for the benefit of their children, their grandchildren, and the other descendants of those alive today.

There are only a few of us, I suppose, who are really dedicated to that. Most of us tend to get into a Sancho Panza condition at one time or another—we're so concerned with our own belly, we can't govern ourselves. The higher passions cannot seize us and grip us and sustain us. But those who take pleasure in doing good, will look back at the long history of thousands of years of history before us. They will look back to the great gift which was given to humanity by western European Christian civilization in the form of the Renaissance, and the new institutions which were created.

Those of us who enjoy that, will participate and try to continue that process, and re-live it in its proper form for today, because that, to us, is the greatest pleasure. (I'm 72, I'm not going to be around for much longer, and I'd better get about my business, and decide to get the thing done, that needs to be done by me, because I don't have much time to waste.)

Therefore, my interest lies not in myself as such, but in what I do for mankind. And that is the way you reach the richest harvest in your own life, a thing of which your grandchildren can be proud may be the thing which is most vital to your self-interest and true pleasure today.

And that's what makes a statesman. As de Gaulle said in his *Memoirs,* speaking of the condition in which he took over the leadership of France after the disaster of the Fourth Republic when France was about to disintegrate in its own decadence, he found the French people sitting like calves in the meadow chewing their cud, who mistook the real estate of France, its rivers and mountains and pastures and so forth, for French interests. And he said the true interest of France, was to recognize France's responsibility for the maintenance and improvement of civilization at large, so that France could prove it was a necessary nation for the sake of humanity.

And if each of us can do that, and find that the thing that motivates us, is a recognition of what our necessary duty is toward humanity in our lifetime. That is our true self-interest. The good that we do for others, since we have such short lives, turns out to be our truest self-interest. And our grandchildren and great-grandchildren, will probably share that opinion.

So, it is this conception of mankind which inspired the Renaissance, the few who made the revolution, the good revolution. And, given the condition of mankind, those of us who understand this problem, will have to act as missionaries, and take the responsibility of leadership to bring the poor people of this world into a force that can reestablish the kinds of great institutions which the Renaissance brought us, minus the oppressive oligarchy, such as the Prince Philip and the Club of the Isles entente.

That's where we stand.

The Post-Industrial Debacle

Now, I've indicated what the financial prospects are for us now. I just recommend Figure 1 to your reflection occasionally, to help you recognize what a wonderful gift was given to mankind by the Renaissance, which proved that mankind does not have to live like a beast, either in totality or otherwise. Ninety-five percent of the people do not have to live in brutish toil so that a few can live in privilege.

We've shown in the United States that 2% of the population or less, with modern technology, can, if allowed, feed an entire nation, and part of the rest of the world besides. We have shown that with about 60% of the labor force employed in industry, we can have the highest rate of wealth per capita imaginable, that there is no problem, with the aid of science in this approach, which cannot be addressed. There is a solution waiting for every problem that confronts us out there, if we are mobilized to muster our creativity to solve it.

That is the challenge we must face. That is the problem we must solve. The purpose of today's presentations is to report to you on programs which will aid us in avoiding a long plunge into a world economic depression, programs which rely upon those proven principles which enabled modern western European culture to emerge as a world culture, as the most powerful form of culture which has ever existed.

First of all, I want to introduce to you the way in which the development policies which we will identify here came into being. Some of you know the story. It's of rather historic significance. Some do not. But by identifying it, those who do know it, will put up with the repetition, because it establishes the common ground for understanding.

In 1974, I happened to see something I knew because I had been involved in my professional work in economics in combatting Norbert Wiener, John Von Neumann, and others. So I knew what the New Age was, and how dangerous it was. I saw, in 1964, some proposals, including the so-called "Triple Revolution," which informed me that the most hideous and most evil movement which could be imagined, was about to be unleashed upon the populations of North America and western Europe, as a mass recruiting project: what

became known as the counterculture, the New Age, "post-industrial society."

So, I didn't know what to do. I was only an individual. I was a management consultant privately. I'd worked for corporations, management consulting firms, and I was largely working with people I knew, on projects. What could I do?

In about 1966, I had the opportunity to teach, and I got into teaching. And I found myself getting into trouble, because a good number of young people seemed to like what I was doing, and what are we going to do about this. Well, all I was trying to do, was to try to intervene on the campuses, hoping that I could help rescue a few talented minds from the garbage that was about to be dumped on those minds.

So, we began to fight on practical issues. I was concerned about poverty in the United States, how it was unnecessary, how it could be understood. Research projects were done by these students, university students, some graduate students. This woman here [moderator Nancy Spannaus] was a student at that time in social work, graduate work at Columbia, and, among others, they did studies of the way the real estate system works in New York, how the tenants are looted in New York City. And they came up with a conclusive case, and learned a good deal in the process. Others did other things.

We organized around the point which I was committed to, of course, as a matter of course, being a World War II veteran, that the solution for the problems of the United States, was that the United States must make a commitment to the technological development of the developing sector. This, even in the narrowest way, would be advantageous to the United States, because if you have a company, and you're manufacturing a product, you don't believe in killing your customers. As a matter of fact, you try to sell them products which will make them more prosperous, because then they'll buy more products. And that was the way we proposed it.

We said, "The people of the developing nations, if they're given the opportunity through infrastructure and investments to develop their own economies, will become bigger customers. So isn't it very stupid to keep them poor, to keep your customers bankrupt? That's not a very good business practice." So, we organized around that.

Well, we got into a lot of trouble, but just to make short and get to this point. In April 1975, I was invited to go to Iraq and spend several weeks there. The occa-

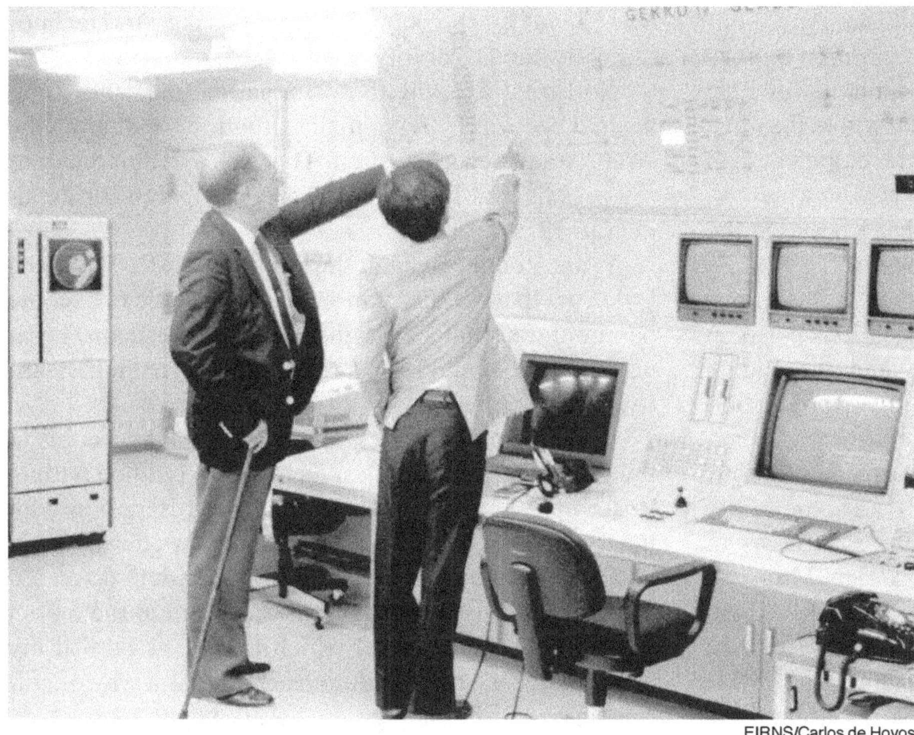

Lyndon LaRouche in the control room of the GEKKO XII laser fusion machine, at the Institute for Laser Engineering at Osaka University in Japan. Third World nations were told to wait for access to high technology, and then were told, "No," by Prince Philip and his minions.

sion of the visit was the Ba'ath Party had its anniversary of its formation every year in April, and I went there, because I liked the opportunity of talking to the Iraqis, finding out what they're up to, and talking also with many other Arabs and others, who were there, from every part of the Arab world, the Islamic world. And we had some wonderful conversations, and I expressed my views.

I told them that Lebanon was about to be divided by civil war, which some fellows in London and Henry Kissinger were about to unleash. And they said, "No, that can't happen, we've got the situation under control." I said, "You don't know London and Henry Kissinger." And while we were there, in Iraq, if some of you are old enough to remember that, the civil war in Lebanon broke out, orchestrated from London, with weapons supplied in part by Kissinger through the State Department.

Organizing for Mideast Peace

So, they became very interested in what I had to say, in that circumstance, and we began to talk about some other things, and I expressed my ideas on a number of subjects, including Arab-Israeli peace. I stated that the only possible basis for peace in a situation such as that between the Israelis and the Palestinians, is to find a common interest, and the only common interest which existed in that circumstance, considering the bloody bitterness which had erupted—it's like the Northern Ireland situation and other situations around the world—is a vital common interest in economic development of the region, to mutual benefit.

If people can share, as separate sovereign peoples, the idea of co-operation to mutual benefit, including economic development to improve the lives of their people, that common interest can be the mortar which puts the bricks together, and makes peace possible. It doesn't guarantee it, but it makes it possible.

The Arabs said, "Well, if you can pull it off, and get these guys together, we're all for it."

So, when I left Baghdad, on the way home, I decided to make a detour into Germany, to get some jobs done in Europe. So I went to my friends in Germany, and we organized around that, and we had a big mobilization, including a couple of press conferences I gave. My wife was involved in this at the time. We mobilized two things: a general international economic development program to counter the effects of the Rambouillet type of process, of Azores conference; and also, special efforts with both Israelis, the sane Israelis, and our friends in the Palestine Liberation Organization, to see if we could put this together and get some negotiations between Israelis and Palestinians going again on this idea of economic development. Because economic development, *then as now,* in the context of Middle East peace, is vital to the peace of the world.

The Middle East will be an area between Israelis and Arabs, or among Arabs and Arabs. It is the crossroads of civilization. It is where the Mediterranean, which is the heart of Europe, meets the Indian Ocean, which is the gateway to the Indian and Pacific Ocean basins. It's the gateway to India, to Pakistan, to Southeast Asia, to China—the greatest concentration of population in the world, including the population of East Africa. This is the future of civilization, where the most people are; that's where the most development can occur.

Therefore, it's important that we have peace in the Middle East, and that we have nations in the Middle East which will administer as their business, the things we need to establish—better communications between the Mediterranean and the Atlantic and the Indian Ocean and Pacific Basin, where the great population concentrations of this planet are located.

I saw that then, and it's clearer, of course, now, when there has been a serious effort. And some of the same forces, the forces around Arafat, the forces in Israel which are associated with [Foreign Minister] Shimon Peres and [Prime Minister Yitzhak] Rabin now, these were the forces we talked to in 1975. In 1976, we were very close to pulling something off. It was very difficult. Not "we," but we as a catalytic agent. Then the Likud government came to power, and it collapsed.

In the 1980s, there were efforts to do the same thing.

In 1976-77, I became aware that what was called "Mutually Assured Destruction," the so-called Kissinger-McNamara policy (really, the Bertrand Russell policy), was actually the road to potential thermonuclear destruction of this planet. During that period, it was obvious to me that the weapons systems in Russia and the United States were more accurate, were forward-based, and that, with the development of techniques such as enhanced radiation effects, the so-called electromagnetic pulse (EMP) effect, that a few thermonuclear warheads exploded over the United States could prevent the land-based missile system of the United States from functioning, and that a Soviet submarine, a boomer or two, situated off the Atlantic and Pacific coasts of the United States, could launch a dozen or half-dozen warheads by missiles over the United States, and the United States was out of business. This gave the President of the United States a matter of a few minutes, at most, to decide whether to "push the button."

The forward-basing of NATO weapons toward the Soviet Union, including the submarine-based weapons, created a similar situation on the other side. And what Kissinger and Robert McNamara hailed as the balance of terror as the key to peace, was actually becoming a hair trigger for the potential of first strike. And technologically, the possibility of a first strike occurred.

So I tried to apply to this situation, the same thing we had been applying to many situations, including the Arab-Israeli peace question. This was a featured part of my presidential Democratic Party campaign for President in 1979-80.

I met Ronald Reagan during that period. We had a little chat there, which caused a lot of people to become paranoid, but that's all right. It's good for them. Paranoid people should have a right to exercise their insanity, occasionally.

The time came when, for various reasons, people in the Reagan government asked me if I would be willing to set up a back-channel, exploratory discussion with the top level of the Soviet government. We discussed it, and I asked them: "How about, if we want to do an exploratory discussion, why don't I present to the Soviet government the proposal which I made as part of my campaign, and see how they react to it, as a way of getting a good discussion going?" And, it was approved.

So, in February 1982, after the agreement was reached to go ahead with this, I organized a conference in Washington, which was actually over two days, on the subject of strategic ballistic missile defense and related problems. Most of the establishment of Washington which is relevant were represented. The intelligence establishment was represented, as were most of the European governments and the Soviet and East bloc governments.

So I put the policy on the table, and then, following that, I met with a Soviet representative in Washington by the name of Yevgeny Shershnev, who is now retired, and we began discussions, where he was reporting to his government what the discussion was, and I was reporting to mine. In the meantime, I was presenting this as an option for discussion.

There was great interest until Andropov was appointed in the summer of 1982 to replace Brezhnev, who was dying. In February 1983, I got a flat turndown on the discussion from the Soviet government, from Andropov, through Shershnev. The point was they agreed that what I had proposed was scientifically sound and militarily sound, but they said the United States would beat the Soviets in a crash program to develop these kinds of systems.

Despite the turndown, the President went ahead with the anti-ballistic missile policy, and it became known as the Strategic Defense Initiative afterward.

The Historical Opportunity of 1989

Now, in my discussion with Shershnev, what I told him he should relay to his principals in Moscow at that February meeting, was that, if the President of the United States were to adopt my proposal, as he did publicly at the end of March 1983, in the famous television broadcast, and if the Soviet government were to reject that, and to follow an independent course along the track that it was already on, then, your economy will collapse. I said, "Your economy, the Soviet system economy, will collapse within about five years. Your best chance, and the best chance for peace, is not to look for affection and love between the superpowers, but to find a basis in mutual interest, particularly the dangerous threat, where we're both being driven to first strike by this silly system which [Bertrand] Russell dreamed up and which Kissinger and McNamara are noted for. You bought it, it was a mistake. The United States government bought it, it was a mistake. We've got to end it, it's dangerous."

So, these were my policies.

Then, in 1989, something happened. I made an address, as part of my presidential campaign for the Democratic nomination in 1988. I made it for reasons which are obvious from what you'll see, in Berlin, at the Kempinski-Bristol Hotel. And this is an excerpt of that address [from the videotape]:

Announcer: "Come with me to Berlin, where I delivered a major press conference on the morning of Wednesday, Oct. 12."

LaRouche: "Under the proper conditions, many today will agree that the time has come for early steps toward the reunification of Germany, with the obvious prospect that Berlin might resume its role as the nation's capital.

"For the United States, as for Germans and Europe generally, the question is: Will this reunification process be brought about by assimilating the Federal Republic into the East bloc's economy, or economic range of influence; or can it be accomplished in a different way? In other words, is a united Germany to come into being as a part of Europe from the Atlantic to the Urals, as President de Gaulle proposed, or as Mikhail Gorbachov has desired: a Europe from the Urals to the Atlantic.

"I see the possibility that the process of unification, could occur precisely as de Gaulle proposed. I base this possibility on the reality of a terrible, worldwide food crisis which has erupted during the past several months, and which will dominate the world's politics in every part of the world, for at least two years to come.

"The economy of the Soviet bloc itself, is a terrible and worsening failure. In western European culture, we have demonstrated that the successes of nations of big industries, depend upon the technologically progressive independent farmer and what is called here in Germany, the *Mittelstand.*

"Soviet culture in its present form is not capable of applying this lesson. Despite all attempts at structural reform, and despite any amount of credit supplied by the foolish West, the Soviet bloc economy as a whole, has reached a critical point. At its present time, in its present form, it will continue to slide downhill from hereon, even if the present worldwide food crisis had not come into being.

"I do not foresee the possibility of genuine peace between the United States and the Soviet Union, earlier than 30-40 years from now. The best we can do in the meantime, in the name of peace, is to avoid a new general war among the major powers. This war avoidance must be based partly upon armed strength and our political will. It must be based also, on rebuilding the strength of our economies.

"At the same time that we discourage Moscow from dangerous military and similar adventures, we must heed the lesson taught to us by a great military scientist from about 400 years ago, Niccolò Machiavelli. We must always provide our adversary with a safe route of escape. We must rebuild our economies to the level at which we can provide the nations of the Soviet bloc an *escape* from the terrible and worsening effects of their economic suffering.

"During 1988, the world will have produced between 1.4 and 1.7 billion tons of food, of grain, and that is already a disastrous world shortage of grain. To ensure conditions of political and strategic stability during 1989 and 1990, we shall require between 2.4 and 2.5 billion tons of grain worldwide, approximately. At those levels we will be able to meet *minimal* Soviet requirements; without something approaching that level, we could not."

What happened, of course, after that address (this was an excerpt of the address, which was broadcast nationwide during the campaign that October), was that, as we subsequently discovered, the Soviet forces were mobilized in East Germany in 1989, to overrun western Europe.

That is, until the Berlin Wall actually fell in late 1989, Moscow was prepared for a military launch, an overrun of western Europe, including the British (which probably would have been fair to them, but I didn't want the rest of the people to suffer).

At the same time, of course, the Wall did fall, and it fell for exactly the reasons that I told Shershnev in 1983, and for the reasons I indicated in that address in Berlin and similar things elsewhere.

So, my response to the fall of the Wall, particularly in discussions with my wife, who did a great deal of the work on this, and who will tell you something about that from her eyewitness experience; she shook the world up a little bit on this one. She can do that. Don't let her deceive you. She can do that. She shakes me up, occasionally.

My response, was to propose what became known in English as the "Productive Triangle" proposal.

This is the document which was later published (**Figure 2**) which contained (it's a fairly thick document) the plans for a general economic development of Eurasia, starting from an area in Europe, which I called the Productive Triangle.

I want to give a physical-geographic image of this (**Figure 3**). There is an area from Paris, which runs down to Vienna, which runs across Bohemia, into Berlin. From Berlin, it runs back above the Ruhr, and above Lille in France, to Paris.

This area of Europe is the most highly developed area of the world. It has the greatest productive potential, in terms of infrastructure, of the world. It has inland waterways, which were started by Charlemagne, on a large scale. We just completed, in 1990, I believe, the last leg of the Rhine-Main-Danube Canal, which was projected by Charlemagne in that period, nearly 1,200 years earlier.

It has the highest concentration of rail transport, per square kilometer. It has the greatest volume of ton-mile-hours of distribution of freight. It has the highest concentration of productive power potential of any part of the world.

Therefore, my proposal was: develop the Productive Triangle, and run from the Productive Triangle (**Figure**

FIGURE 3

European 'Productive Triangle'

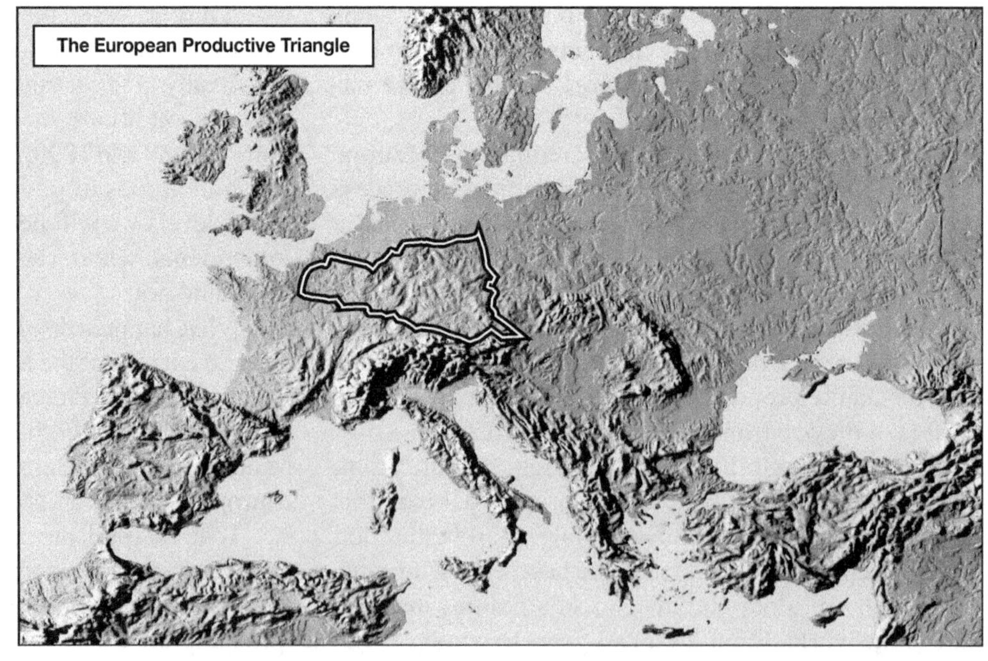

4), from Berlin, from Vienna, from Paris, what are like the stellar spiral arms of a spiral galaxy. These spiral arms will include high-speed modern rail, preferentially, magnetic levitation rail, including through the development of better superconductors, heavy freight carriage by this high-speed substitute for rail, magnetic levitation. This means [travel speeds of] 300 miles an hour. This means the virtual elimination of air transport, air traffic congestion, for passenger flights, because if you can travel 300 miles an hour, along the route from Boston, Massachusetts down to beyond Washington and Richmond, who's going to take a plane? You can get there cheaper and safer and quicker by rail or by magnetic levitation than you can by air.

So, develop that system. In the same way, use our inland waterways. Western Europe is rich in standard inland waterways. Barge traffic is the cheapest method of inland freight, especially for bulk freight, for agricultural commodities, for heavy ore, sand, whatever.

There is almost *no* development; there are some big things in Russia, but no general development in eastern Europe of an adequate system of inland waterways, to enable us to have low-cost bulk freight. There's almost no rail system capable of handling the needs of a modern economy.

In western Europe, the Triangle has a great concentration of productive power, energies, including, in France, nuclear energy, and some in Germany. So you want to put up an industry? That's the ideal place in the world to put it, or was at that time. You've got the labor, you've got the power, you've got the transportation, rail transport, cheap truck transport. This is very efficient— though very costly, much more costly than rail—but efficient on short hauls. Also readily available are barge transport, power, sanitation, labor force, educational facilities, and so forth.

The region of the Productive Triangle is the best place in the world to invest. We must begin to develop the areas down through the Balkans, into Italy, into North Africa.

Go to Warsaw from Berlin. From Warsaw, go to St. Petersburg; from the same area, go to Moscow. Go down to Ukraine, to Kiev, and so forth, and so on. And move further. Build across Asia.

The Franco-Russian Alliance

This is not a new fantasy. This was actually proposed, in a general way, in the 1890s, by a Russian, Count Sergei Witte, the foreign minister and government leader, at times, in Russia, who was politically a follower of the great Russian ally of Abraham Lincoln, Alexander II; who was a collaborator of Dmitri Mendeleyev, the discoverer of the Periodic Table, the great chemist; who also built the railroads of Russia, such as they were. And did some other things; Vernadsky was one of his students.

And then in France you had Leo XIII, the pope, and a French politician, who was better than the average French politician, though I have a lot of complaints about him. His name was Gabriel Hanotaux. And Gabriel Hanotaux and Witte shaped a policy, to build a network of rail and other infrastructure developments, across from Brest in France, to Vladivostok and into Japan, by modern rail systems. The next step was to take these rail systems down into China, to build a rail network from Berlin into Baghdad, and so forth and so on.

This was the cause of World War I, because the British didn't want this to happen.

The point is: We've had hell in Europe since that time, since the beginning of this century. In 1989, the Berlin Wall dropped, the division of Europe, the amputation of Europe from itself by the Wall, by the communist divide, had ended, or at least partly. This was the great opportunity, to take this vastly underdeveloped part of this planet of Eurasia from Berlin to the East, into Japan, down into China, linked to India, and in turn, the rest of Asia, which is the greatest concentration of the world's population, into a workshop of great productivity. And obviously, where you have the most people, you can get the greatest benefit from improvement in productivity, as in China, or India.

So that was my proposal, with my knowledge of modern technology. The assumption is that we could bring these nations into a new era of development.

You know, it's like a death in the family, when even a communist regime falls. The people are living in shock, they're living in a sense of freedom. It is necessary to act then, in some way, to establish a sense of stability under these conditions of shock. And if you can stretch the hand of friendship and cooperation to those people at that time, you may be able to bring about a great good, which it would not be possible to win them to, under other circumstances.

That was our objective. Unfortunately, the British had other ideas.

Today's Problem

Now, let me just indicate what the problem has been and what the problem is today, in politics.

In November 1989, directly contrary to what I was proposing, Mrs. Margaret Thatcher, who is a fascist, began to scream about German reunification. Thatcher is a protégé of the Mont Pelerin Society, has the ideas of the Mont Pelerin Society, the ideas which came out of that brand of fascism, which is associated with Friedrich von Hayek, and those types of people, the type of fascism which is advocated by Phil Gramm, the senator in the United States, and, in a sense, by Newt Gingrich.

I know these people very well. As a matter of fact, they've got an Auschwitz program for privatization of the prison system. They really do match up with the Nazis on these kinds of things.

Thatcher began to scream, together with the same Conor Cruise O'Brien who was her lackey at that point, who just caused the fall of the Irish government, in an effort by the British intelligence service to prevent the Northern Ireland peace from functioning. They began screaming, and said the unification of Germany would constitute an economic threat to the vital interests of Great Britain. It would be a Fourth Reich. It would link up with Russia. It would open up Eurasia—they didn't say this, but they meant it: German reunification represents the same threat to British imperial interests that Hanotaux and Witte represented in the 1890s.

What the British have done so far, and during the previous administration with George Bush in full cooperation, is to repeat exactly the same policy which the British used, to create World War I. And I do not exaggerate. People will tell you something else from the history books, but they don't know what they're talking about.

Here's how it happened. By 1896, Hanotaux and Witte had cemented a number of nested agreements, which would have established these Eurasian economic cooperation projects, to help free China from the grip of the British, through aid of economic development, and to bring in the cooperation of the Japanese.

At that time, prior to 1901 and the assassination of President William McKinley, the United States had been allied, since the time of Lincoln, with three major powers outside the United States: one, Prussia, or Germany; two, Russia; and three, Meiji Restoration Japan.

With the assassination of McKinley and British agent Teddy Roosevelt brought into power, that shifted. The United States' close relations with those countries was broken; and the United States established a close relationship with Britain.

The Entente Cordiale

But something else happened in the meantime.

In Africa, the policy of England at the time, was to run a railroad as a method of conquest from Cairo to Cape Horn. The area which was at risk in this, was what we call today, Sudan. The French policy in that period, was to run a railroad (as it had been from the 1870s on), from Dakar (what we today call Senegal), to Djibouti, in East Africa, a sub-Sahel rail line, which would run through the areas we'd call Nigeria (Nigeria, Chad, and so forth), across Sudan, and across what we'd call Ethiopia or Abyssinia, to Djibouti.

This was 1898. The British were ready to go to war with France on this issue. Lord Kitchener came onto the scene, along with the grandfather of Boutros-Boutros Ghali, who was called Boutros *Pasha* Boutros-Ghali, and was a great assassin of Sudanese people in that time (and, I guess, the present U.N. secretary general maintains that tradition as a British lackey who likes to assassinate Africans). Lord Grey from London controlled a French politician by the name of Théophile Delcassé, and the so-called *revanchiste* faction in France.

Delcassé cut an order, ordering a French captain who was in the area, one Captain Marchand, to surrender to Kitchener. And the policy of France was changed, so that France became the lackey of England from that point on, in an arrangement which became known as the Entente Cordiale, the relationship between a sodomite and a catamite.

The Entente Cordiale was consolidated in 1904. In 1905, the British began organizing the Russian Revolution. Actually, they had already organized it, but in 1905 they called it into action to bring down Witte. Witte's power in Russia was destroyed by the 1905 Revolution, just as a lot of Russian industry was destroyed, and the Baku oil fields. At the same time, the British, through the Dreyfus scandal, and through the surrender of the French at Fashoda in Sudan, ordered by Delcassé, when Marchand surrendered to Kitchener, made France a captive of London.

The British owned the Serbians. The Serbians of that period were complete puppets of the British, *as they are today.* This is not something new, this is an old story. The British had a freemasonic lodge in Salonika.

This freemasonic lodge was called International B'nai B'rith. The International B'nai B'rith Lodge in Salonika became a government of Turkey, called the "Young Turk" government. Vladimir Jabotinsky, the founder of the Israeli Likud, was the editor of the newspaper of the Young Turk government.

On this basis, they induced Bulgaria to find itself at war with Greece, and, with the aid of Serbia, set into motion a series of Balkan wars which ultimately became World War I. In the process of this, with Witte out of power, the British managed to manipulate their assets in Russia to activate a Slavophile faction, to move in support of Britain's puppet Serbia, against the Croatians, Slovenians, Bosnians, and so forth, as they have done today. Out of this arrangement, the British organized what became known as the Triple Entente. World War I began when the Russian Army was called up in a general mobilization for the purpose of launching a war, a military attack on Austro-Hungary and Germany.

The Germans attempted to get the Russians to call off the mobilization, because the mobilization would require *them* to mobilize. The Russians refused to call off the mobilization, the Germans mobilized; and World War I was on.

What Mrs. Thatcher and George Bush did, *was the same thing.* Thatcher organized, with [President François] Mitterrand and other forces in France, a revival, as the British press and British government said, of the Entente Cordiale. The same faction of British intelligence today says this openly; the same faction is out to kill President Clinton, and that's a fact. They are organizing a Triple Entente with Moscow, against Germany in the lesser part, but primarily against the United States.

The Destruction of Eastern Europe

Instead of opening up eastern Europe, Russia, Ukraine, and so forth to development, as we should have done, which would have led to the greatest economic boom in this planet's history, if we'd done it, what they did, was to impose so-called reform, through a virtual British-shared puppet, Mikhail Gorbachov, and his successor, who has the same politics, Boris Yeltsin.

As a result of these reforms in Poland, in the Czech Republic, in Hungary, Romania, and Ukraine, the level of per capita, per square kilometer, and per household production of wealth, in the former Soviet bloc, is now today *less than 30% of what it was in 1989.*

What you have in these countries, are former U.S. Ambassador to the U.S.S.R. Bob Strauss's friends, a mafia composed of elements of the old state apparatus, which is stealing the country blind from the inside in Russia, and hawking the proceeds for nickels, like people who steal television sets out of your apartment, on the streets of London, for pennies. Russia is being bled dry. Poland is being looted dry. The Czech economy, which is the so-called glorious example of reform, is in dangerous trouble. Hungary is suffering.

The British, in order to prevent development, in 1991 launched their Serbian fascist puppets (and Serbian President Slobodan Milosevic is *owned* by the British psychological warfare division), first of all against Croatia and Slovenia, then against Bosnia-Hercegovina, with the intention to broaden the war generally.

The United Nations, through the Franco-British Entente Cordiale, and a British agent as U.N. secretary general, and a Yeltsin who is playing ball with the British (up to a point, he may be overthrown any minute, who knows, he's not long for this world), have orchestrated a bloody war, and have run the war as a war against the present government of the United States. Not a shooting war against us; but every Bosnian shot, is really a bullet aimed at the policy of the United States government.

If this continues in eastern Europe, you can imagine what the consequences could be. The Russians have not been conquered by anyone since they escaped the Mongol occupation in the course of the fifteenth century. They have not been conquered. They are not a people like some of the other nations of Europe, who are used to being defeated and occupied for a time by other powers. They have a distinct culture, with distinct problems, and they cannot accept defeat.

These idiots in London and in Washington and elsewhere, are driving the Russian people and the Russian military and other forces into a state of desperation which can lead to an explosion. They are committing crimes in the Balkans, with the endorsement and backing of the British government and the French government and the United Nations, which are *crimes as bad as those committed in the field, by any stretch of the imagination, by the Nazis in World War II.*

What they are doing in Africa, is worse. But that doesn't make the headlines. What they are doing in other parts of the world, is similar. And so *that is our problem.*

We can fix it, still, if we can stretch out the hand of friendship and economic cooperation to these troubled areas of the world. We will say, "Look, we're all in trouble, terrible mistakes have been made. *Let's fix it.*" And we can have peace. And that's what I'm at.

I believe in the principles which I tried with the Arab-Israeli peace, which are very important to me, that Mr. Peres and Mr. Rabin pulled off as well as they did; because that is a touchstone of an example of what can be done in the way of building peace between peoples who are separated by rivers of blood. And if you can build peace between people who are separated by rivers of blood, you can build peace anywhere, through economic and related cooperation. To solve hunger, to solve the problems of the individual, of the family household, and so forth.

Okay, we have the political map of Europe. We've gone through this. And you know the Ninth Forecast [pamphlet published by LaRouche's 1996 presidential exploratory committee (**Figure 2**)]. In this pamphlet, I indicate what I described before, the nature of the impending global financial and monetary collapse.

Build Infrastructure

So, the question is: Given these facts, what do we do? And one would hope that we could induce some people around Washington and elsewhere, to support the President of the United States, and to push such a policy now.

Forget the fact that this system is going to blow. My policy, in every part of the world, is to build infrastructure. When our friends or governments or other people ask us, "What shall we do?" I say, "Start the infrastructure-building projects now. Start them on a small scale, because you have to start large projects on a small scale, to bring together the cadres of people who are going to do the job, and then you can expand the project on a larger scale, once you've got a nucleus which is functioning and is a proven administration and initial core."

They should be done in all parts of the world. Water systems: in Africa, for example, fresh well water, potable well water, is a crucial factor. You can always do something good, in every part of the world, if you just put your mind to it. Let's get these projects going, especially large railway, pipeline, power line, infrastructure-building corridors.

The way we finance this is simple. When we go into a bankruptcy, as we will, either through chaos or through orderly bankruptcy, it is obvious that anybody who is talking about free trade, *has to be a lunatic,* living in virtual reality. Because when the central financial and monetary systems of the world are in bankruptcy reorganization, there is no large source of private capital for large-scale investments. In a bankruptcy reorganization, you're lucky to keep the doors open. You do not have abundant internal resources.

There's only one way you can approach this effectively, and that is to replace the present world system of central banking, that is, central banks controlled by private interests, like the Federal Reserve System, which is charted by the federal government, but it's owned by private financial interests. They have a monopoly over our money and credit, not the government. If you want to cure the problem of the burdens of taxes, put the Federal Reserve System back into bankruptcy, and you'll find out how wonderfully the problem can begin to be solved.

We saw that with the way that George Washington and Alexander Hamilton solved the problem of a bankrupt United States in 1789-91. Go to Article I of the U.S. Constitution. The Congress of the United States has the authority, under the Constitution, of a monopoly on the creation of money.

So, what do you do? You can get the money you will need in the United States for projects as I indicated, about $1-2 trillion, just to get the United States moving in public works and related projects, to keep it from going into a depression.

You put the money into a depository called a national banking institution, which is connected to all the significant banks in the country. This institution loans this money to approved investments, such as by federal, state and local public utilities. These public utilities can borrow at the preferred rate, and they get payment on the same basis that a building contractor gets progress payments for salaries, payroll, and for materials, as he goes along and does phase-in of the job. That way, you're not putting a big chunk of money into circulation, except as the work is done.

So then you have contractors who go to work as bidders who win contracts to assist these agencies in building these projects. They, too, get credit, the way we used to give credit out for war contracts. When you got a war contract, you could take it to a bank, and you could discount that contract for lending, and you could get the money to keep your project going.

On that basis, by putting $2 trillion, for example, into circulation in the United States—*through work,* not through throwing money out in the street—you then generate the basis for a general revival of the U.S. economy. And that is the *only way* that any part of the world is going to recover from the kind of crisis which we're going into now.

There is no hope of getting out of this crisis, until we get rid of central banking, and replace it with a kind of national banking which the United States used in its first federal administration, to get the United States out of bankruptcy, to become one of the most prosperous, productive economies in the world. That, of course, was also used in Germany with Friedrich List.

So, that is the authority which the Congress has under Article I, the authority which the President can invoke with the consent of Congress to provide the money as credit through national banking, to get essential projects going. And we have a need for massive rail, power, and water projects, as well as cleaning up these cesspools which we call our cities in the United States today. Remember, an urban community is a piece of infrastructure. And if it's rundown and destroyed, it's just like a railroad or a water system, or a sanitation system broken down. You cannot have industry, you cannot have production, without these kinds of things.

So, that's the method around the world.

The Great Projects

Now, on that basis, let me indicate what some of these projects are. What we proposed originally, of course, was to go from the Triangle in Europe, across Eurasia. This has two features.

Back in 1983-84, we did a proposal which is called the Indian-Pacific basin development program, which addressed the fact that the Pacific region, with the Indian Ocean region, its littoral, will become the center of the world economy in the coming century. That's where the population is concentrated. If you look at North America, South America, Central America, bounding on the East; you look at Africa, East Africa, bounding on the West; if you consider the Antilles, Japan, Taiwan, and so forth, the Philippines, down into Southeast Asia, Indonesia, Malaysia, and so forth. The Indian subcontinent.

In China, you're talking about over 1.2 billion people in that region. You're talking about a similar, actually a larger number, in South Asia, if you include Pakistan, Bangladesh, India, in that region. You're talking about something going up toward a half-billion people in Southeast Asia alone.

Look at the population of the United States and Canada, the population of the nations which are on the Pacific Coast of South America. You envisage a new sea-level canal through the region of Panama, which brings the Atlantic into the Pacific much more efficiently than now, and you can see very quickly that with high-speed ships using new techniques, magneto-hydrodynamic drives, we now have a completely new picture of the world, in which the maps no longer center around the Atlantic Ocean, as they used to, but the maps of the world center about the Pacific Ocean, and the Indian Ocean. So now, Europe has access to this region, through the Mediterranean, the canal, and the Middle East.

The object is to build a land bridge to and from Europe into China, into Japan, and into Southeast Asia, so that the littoral development, the coastal waterway system in Eurasia, in Asia in particular, is supplemented and integrated with a rail bridge situation.

Now, there are three rail bridges from China into Europe (**Figure 4**). One goes North directly, to intersect, through Kazakhstan, the trans-Siberian artery. Another goes along a more southerly route through Iran, and goes up into Turkey. A third route, goes down, through a link, through an area where I served back during World War II, into the area near Bamu from Kuoming. And that link goes across to Dakar in Bangladesh, goes across into Egypt, across that region.

So, there are three major rail arteries potentially from China into Europe, and vice versa.

This means that the entire area of Siberia, if we do some major engineering on freshwater, and there's plenty there, the center of water for Eurasia is right there, if we do major engineering, then this whole area opens up seriously for development; and the development of trade, power, inland waterways, and so forth, ensures that.

Obviously, this kind of planning has to be controlled in some way. You have to have some scorecard, some meters and measuring devices to determine what works and what doesn't work. Generally, I use my specialty,

Eurasian Land Bridge (The Silk Route)

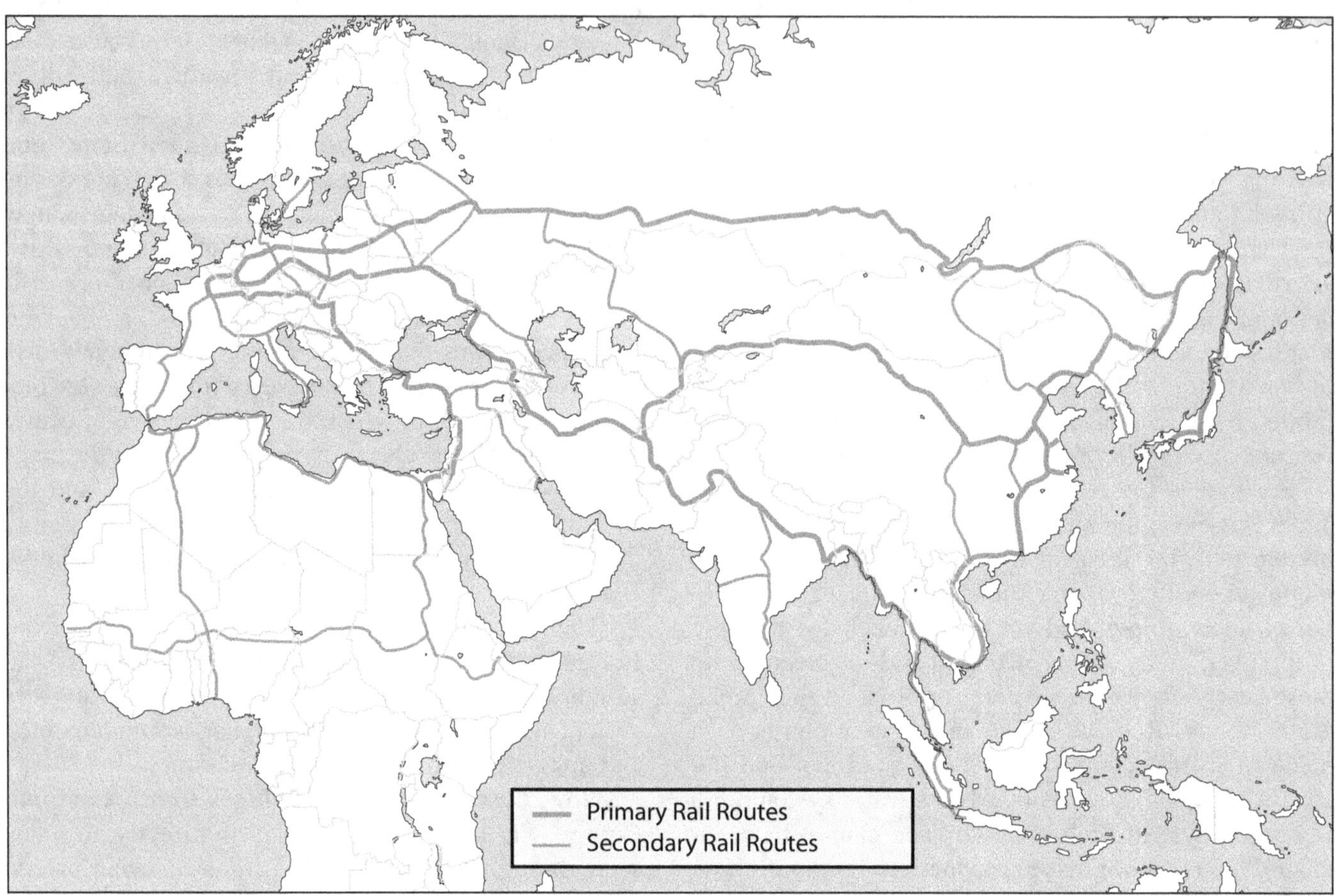

which is called physical economy. In physical economy, we may use prices in a certain phase of our work, but we do not base our estimates of national performance on prices. We study the flow of price movements, but we do not base the estimate of the performance of the economy on prices.

What we base it on, is values of essential consumption, in infrastructure by producers, essentially, and by households, of material consumption, the material consumption required to maintain a certain standard of living, which generally corresponds with a certain level of technological development, *plus* education, plus the health care, plus the science and related services.

That is what people consume, that's what industries consume, that's what infrastructure consumes: physical product plus these things. We measure the market basket per capita and per family of consumption, we measure the consumption in industry per capita, we measure the productivity in these terms per capita, in the labor force.

We measure that in terms of per capita for labor force, household, including accounting for household demography, and also per square kilometer. We measure things like ton-mile-hours against relative physical cost, from media of transportation, such as inland waterways, ocean freight, coastal freight; that sort of thing.

And we measure also the water, in terms of liters or cubic meters per capita, per hour, and so on and so forth, for human consumption, for industry; and the water requirements of a society *increase* as the level of productivity increases.

We measure not only the kilowatt hours of energy required for a level of technology and productivity. We must measure what was called the energy-flux density of that power. As you go to much higher technologies, you acquire better-focused power at higher localized energy-flux densities. Higher energy-flux densities of the type you get with hydrogen fusion, for example, give you much higher, vastly higher efficiency throughout your entire system, than you could get with a low-temperature source of heat.

So, all these factors are taken into account.

We will then figure out what the price is of a wage, and we will then trace the price movement of trading and so forth through the economy, but we measure primarily in physical economy.

Measuring Economies

Now, therefore, in measuring, we have two things to do. I won't go into the details here, but indicate that the basic way in which you measure economy and physical economy is by what is called a *system of inequalities*—what has to relatively increase, what has to relatively decrease. But you must scale it. So, what I had to do years ago, was to define an approximate scaling.

When it comes to scaling, if you want to build a

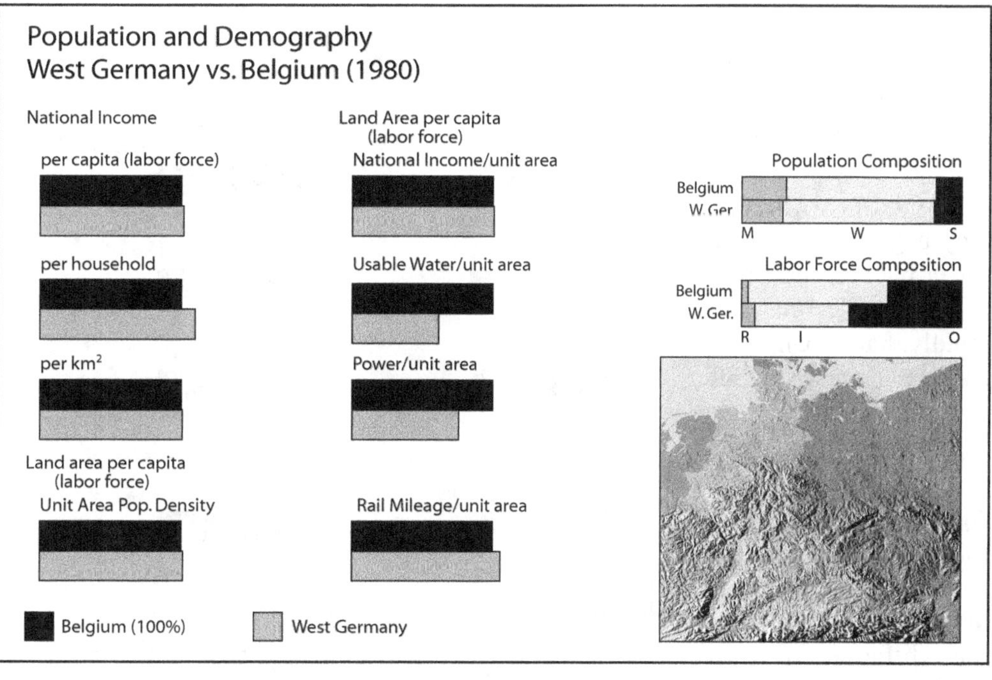

FIGURE 5

FIGURE 6

ruler, you can pick an arbitrary measure, if it's a linear ruler. You can make your ruler up of anything: cubits, feet, centimeters, whatever you want to make it of. Except it has to be consistent.

Now you go out and measure things, and that's

called scaling. What I needed, was a standpoint of reference for scaling economies upon which this kind of long-range planning among different kinds of economies and different conditions, could be correlated without subjecting them to these so-called misleading price calculations.

So, what I did, was to take three economies which were industrialized, and two which were underdeveloped. The three I chose which were industrialized were Japan, West Germany, and the United States. As my baseline, I used 1967-69. The reason I chose those years, is that at that time, the technology and productivity of the three economies was at the same level, approximately, because after 1968-69, the U.S. economy began going into the sewer bucket, and Europe began to decline more rapidly than Japan, so disparities developed after that.

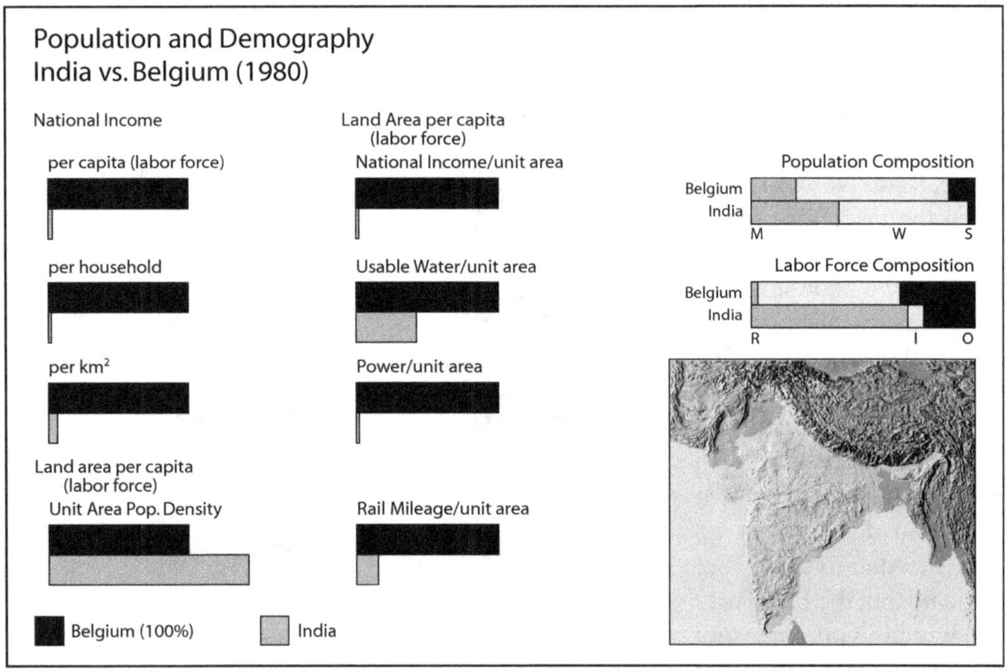

I then compared 1967-69 with 1980 figures. Against these three industrialized economies, each having different population densities and therefore different infrastructural characteristics, I compared the two major developing economies: China and India.

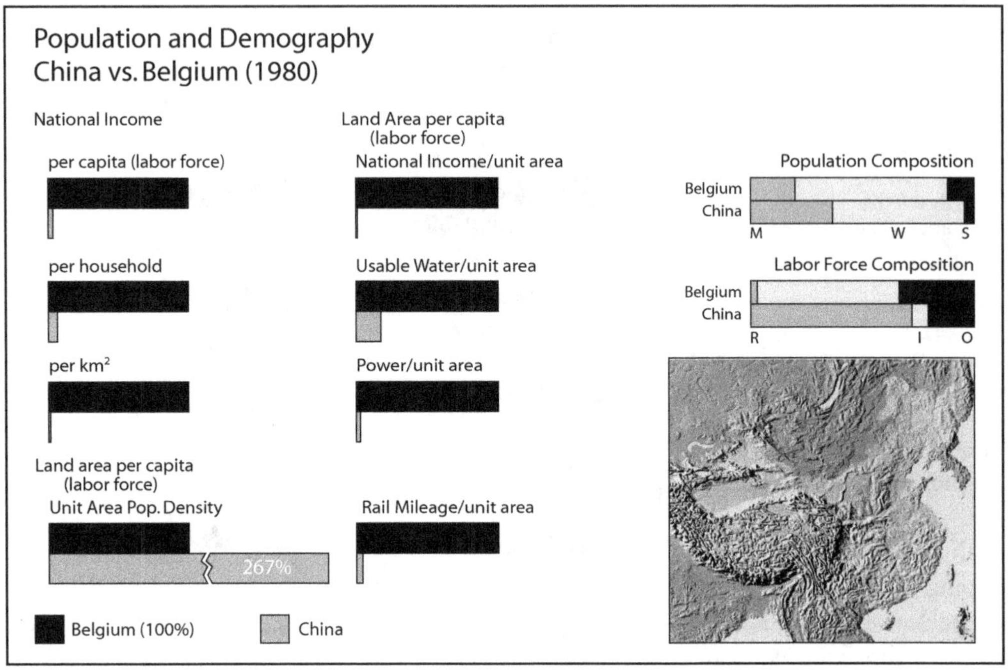

Therefore, by exploring the *gap in development* between India and China on the one side, and these three industrialized countries on the other, I established an arbitrary ruler of arbitrary length, to compare different economies around the world, and to reference which one is improving, and which one is going into the bucket, so to speak.

So, that's what these are.

FIGURE 8

FIGURE 9

I'll just run through these slowly, so people can see (**Figures 4-8**). You see the factors we've listed here, just to give some indication. The world is *not* overpopulated. If you want to say the world is overpopulated, you should go first of all to Singapore or Hongkong, but then you would go to Belgium.

Africa, by the way, is vastly underpopulated. If somebody tells you differently, they don't know what they're talking about. As a matter of fact, there's vast agricultural land there, if it were developed, if people had fresh water, if babies could live long enough to have babies. Things like that.

So, these are the kinds of measures we used, a set of inequalities, plus, as a yardstick, a comparison with Belgium as a common unit of relevance, comparison. And comparing Japan, Germany, and the United States with China and India, because in that, you will find all the problems stated that you need to know, in studying how things are going in the western world.

What we really need to know is, for a level of technology and productivity, what standard of living do you have to provide for a household to sustain that productivity? What standard of living do you have to have, to maintain a demographic model which will make the economy work?

If you have an economy in which the altitude is life-expectancy by years, the baseline is the percentile of the population in that age interval. If you get into economies like very poor developing economies, it's a very flat triangle.

In the case of China, what they're trying to do, is to make it like that, so you have almost no babies, and a lot of old people. So the solution is to control your problem by killing the old people, which is pretty much the idea that Newt Gingrich has for the United States these days.

The point is, in this case, there is a tremendously large population in Asia, admittedly poorly educated in large part, in particular the part we have to reach. But also the land is very poor, and, when someone says, "We don't want to invest in infrastructure, we just want to put industries out there," take them to the nearest loony-bin, get them canvas waistcoats, the ones that tie the arms behind or something, and just keep them out of economics, because the *first requirement of any modern industry* is an adequate development of infrastructure, transportation, ton-miles-per-hour. That sort of thing. Measured per square kilometer.

Water: liters per square kilometer per capita per household.

Power: kilowatt hours.

Energy flux-density: same thing, for each mode of production you require.

If these requirements are satisfied in the development of an area, then you have there, provided you have skilled labor, automatically, immediately, the potential for a successful investment, if you have the right cadres to make it work. So the first thing you have to do, is to develop the infrastructure, *first*. (Ideas like the *maquiladoras* along the U.S. border with Mexico, are *insane*. You cannot build a successful, durable plant on top of a cesspool. You get diseases that way, and you get poor infrastructure.)

Then what you do is what we did in the past in every successful development of an industrial economy beginning in the United States itself during the eighteenth century and the nineteenth century: the development of infrastructure—canals, ports, power facilities, rails, sanitation, and good urban organization.

These were the preconditions of the successful industrial revolution, and the successful agricultural revolution. The biggest factor in the American agricultural revolution of the postwar period, was the rural electrification program which was started under President Franklin Roosevelt during the 1930s and continued throughout the 1940s. The availability of electricity, the improvement of transportation, and so on. Farms (when there was were still farming in this country), per hectare *were greater consumers of steel* than most industries. When they began to liquidate the farm, they were ripping the steel out of the soil, pipeline, everything else. And you had the people who were doing the looting, like Cargill, the great grain cartel trust, which loots the farmers here and loots the farmers in Africa, out there, setting up these melting-down scrap facilities. And a great part of the U.S. steel consumption today is derived from melting down the scrap of the economy, agricultural and industrial, we are destroying.

We are like the man who is having a meal by eating his own left leg.

The 'Productive Triangle'

Now, let's go to the next slide, on this Productive Triangle program (**Figures 10-12**). This is self-explanatory. What we did, is we took the existing rail routes in Europe. Helga [Zepp-LaRouche] can describe this. She was involved in this, heavily. And we proposed the new routes that had to be added.

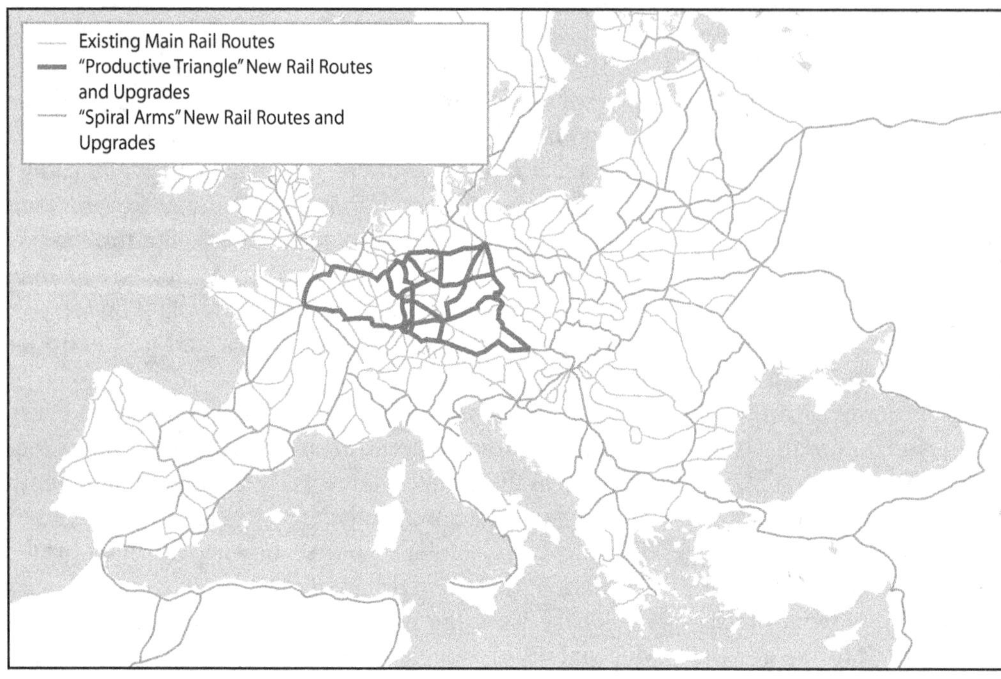

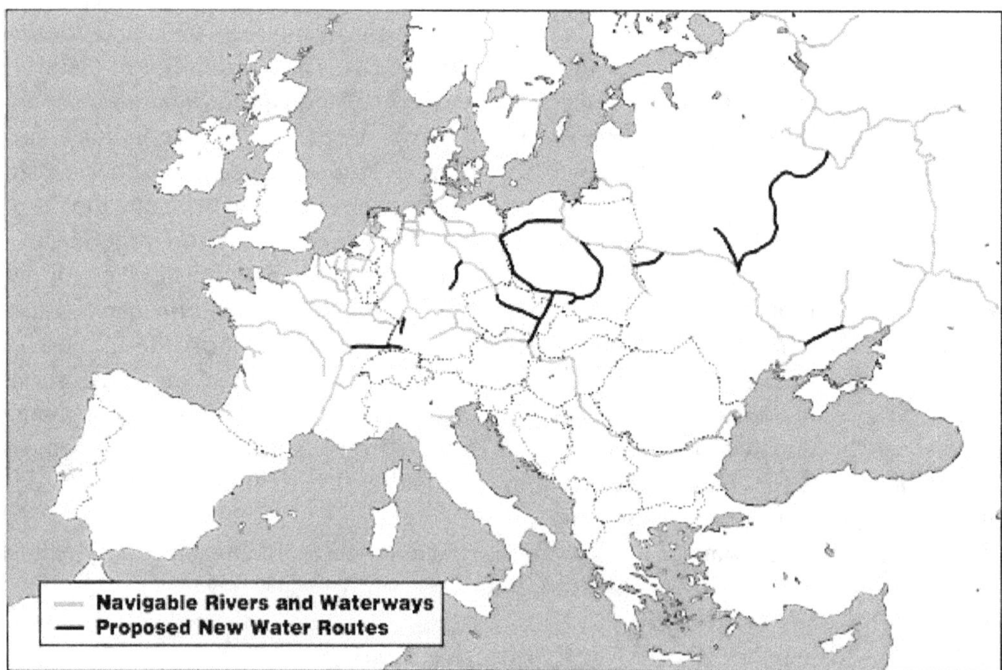

a limited access, even though Russia has giant rivers, to the development of the interior of the country.

So, without new canals, without new rail systems, it's impossible to develop Russia and it's impossible to solve the problems of eastern Europe, and that's also more conspicuous when you get into Asia.

Development of Asia

What we did, is to divide Eurasia into these areas. Take Mongolia and China, with Japan, Korea, and Taiwan, as one unit, because there are natural interrelations among these economies, and therefore, that's a planning unit. You have India and Southeast Asia, which are different, the subcontinent of Southeast Asia, but essentially they also form a planning unit. You have the Middle East area, which is defined by Sudan, the largest country in there. And you have the Central Asian complex, which includes those indicated countries. Then, northern Siberia, which is largely the old Soviet area of Russia, and then eastern and western Europe. Those are the planning areas which we worked on. As you can see we have a mass of slides, but we're limiting what we use today.

We did the same thing with the water system, defined the water systems. You see the difference between western Europe and Russia? What are your chances in competing in productivity with western Europe, in Russia or eastern Europe today? You have

Now, we have the Silk Route railroad. These indicate your routes (**Figure 12**). These are not necessarily precisely accurate. The problem with the Silk

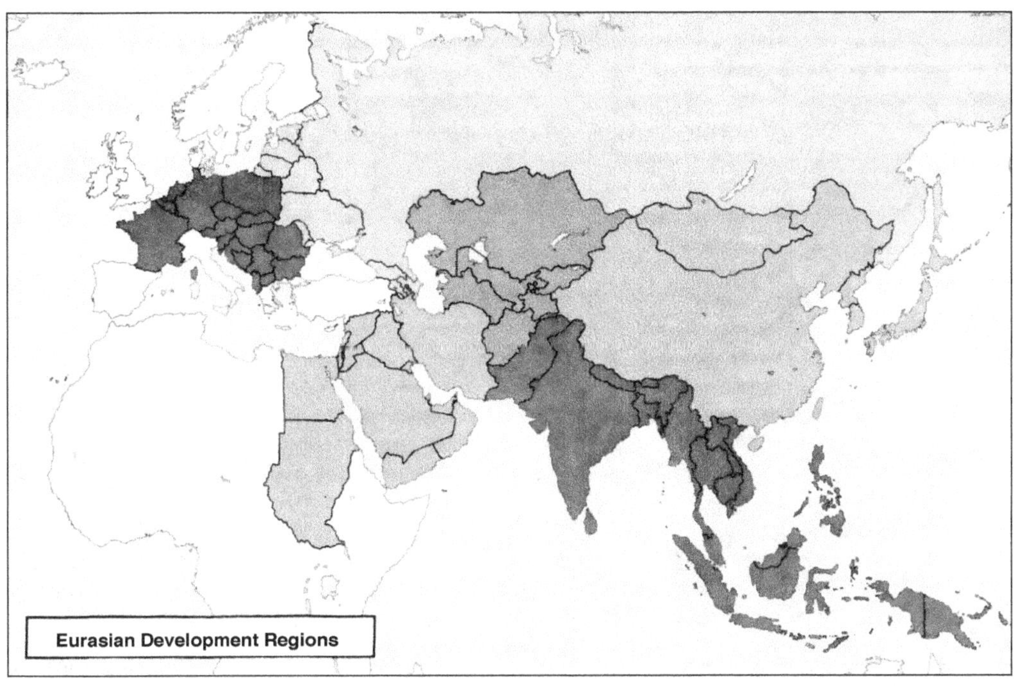

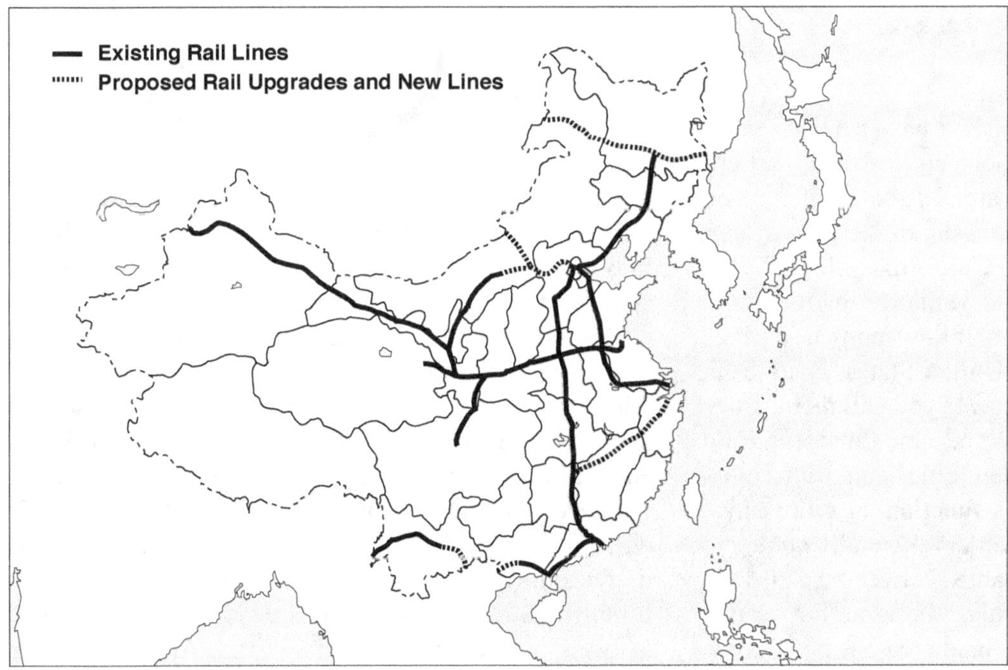

route is obvious.

The middle route which you see there, is obvious. And then there's an indication, though it's not completely drawn on this map, that if you go from Kunming, into this little area where Khun Sa, the drug lord bandit, is now operating in Burma afresh, you'll find there's an area which leads into my old area, Bamo and Mishina, in Burma. This railroad can lead across into Dhaka, in Bangladesh, into India, and then across, into Cairo. So there are these three routes.

The obvious routes, as indicated here, which is already the idea of Hanotaux and Witte, is to make, from Siberia, north of Vladivostok, a rail jump to the islands, and to come down with a rail link into Japan itself, so Japan would be rail-linked into this trans-Asian group. In addition to that, of course, this area is largely an inland sea. One of the interesting features to comment on here, is to look at the island group down there. [See **Figures 13-15** for more detail on the development of Asia.]

The most natural development of Indonesia, will come from the devel-

Route is that it is an area of shifting sands and shifting lakes, and when you try to lay down rail on shifting sands and shifting lakes, you can get some problems. There are surveys which have been done to determine the optimum route, even though the general idea of the opment of water-borne transport. That whole base area there, which we worked some years ago, is water. It's an inland sea. We proposed to cut a canal, which was an old proposal which I got involved in promoting, through the isthmus in Thailand, between the Gulf of Siam, so-called,

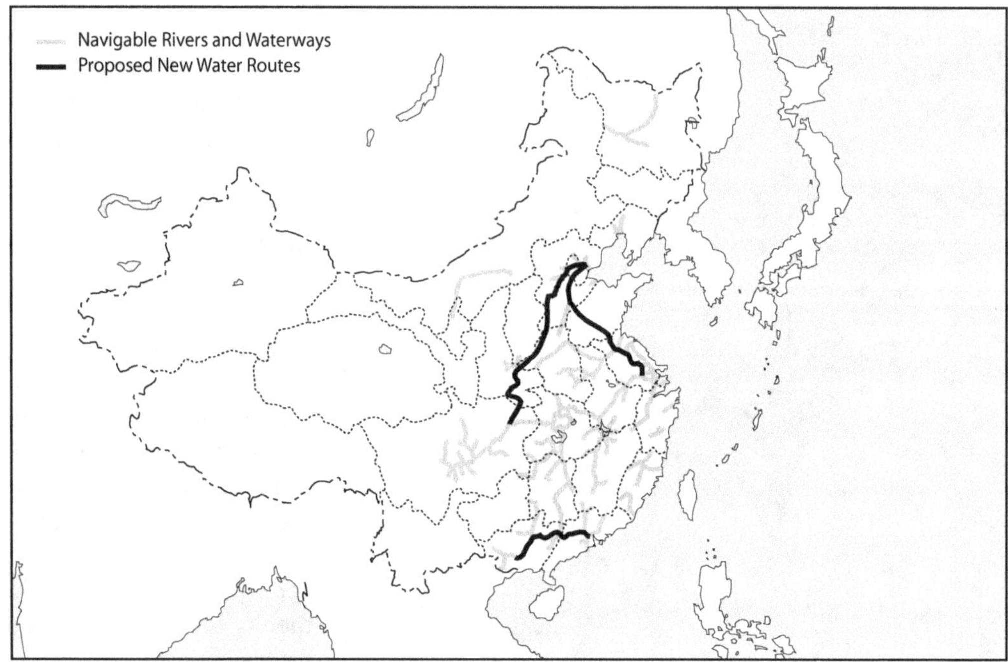

and the Bay of Bengal, which would bring India much more efficiently into this area, and to develop an integrated water-borne economy in that area.

Developing North America

Similarly, in addition to this, we have extensive proposals on North America, which center around particularly developing the eastern area of the Pacific Basin (moving from Japan and Indonesia, to the eastern part of the Pacific Basin which is California, which Teddy Roosevelt shut down). It would be interesting for you to check old maps, and ask yourself how many new cities have been developed in the United States, apart from suburban mushrooms or whatever you call them, since 1911, or since Teddy Roosevelt became President. Find me and tell me how many new cities came into existence in the United States as functioning cities since Teddy Roosevelt became President. Virtually *none*.

Now, look at the western lands, between the 20-inch rainfall line and into California. Show me how much development of this precious land area has been done. You've got people out there in California, idiots, worrying about Proposition 187, about trying to kick the immigrants out. We've got a tremendous amount of land that needs to be developed, right in that area, which is the great American desert, and so forth. *We have the water.* We have the design for the project which would deliver the water where it's needed. We can solve these problems.

We can take our poor youth off the streets, stop them from killing each other, and give them a future in a youth work program to assist in this kind of project. We can do that. We can build new power systems. We can rebuild this country, we can clean up the garbage, and make this country one we're proud of again.

There are great opportunities also in Mexico. Mexico has projects which have never been scratched yet, and they're good projects, I've seen a number of them. They're sound. Colombia has great potential. Venezuela, Brazil, Argentina, Peru. We've done studies on all of these areas. Africa has tremendous potential. We've studied these areas.

There is much work to be done to bring humanity into the kind of condition which would have satisfied my dear friend, Cardinal Nicolaus of Cusa. There's no want of employment. We can do with a lot fewer stockbrokers who do nothing but steal our pension funds and raid our corporations; but we do need skilled people, engineers, scientists, and skilled labor.

We do need the opportunity to take the young children who are destroying each other with drugs and whatnot on the street, and enable them to get a second chance to become real human beings, with work and education and some caring, and a prospect of hope.

We can do that not only in the United States, we can do it in the world. And I've just limned over this, and given some of the concepts which are essential within a time which is already, in a sense, too long, but I wanted to get the essential concepts across. And that's what we're doing.

We know certain things. A lot of things we don't know, a lot of things we have yet to find out. But what we know, we know. And it will work. Shall we say, "I have seen the future and it works"; and it wasn't communism.

www.ingramcontent.com/pod-product-compliance
Lightning Source LLC
Chambersburg PA
CBHW081745250726
48657CB00010B/3407